Healing or Hurting

Caring for Hearts in Broken Bodies

Andrew Davies

malcolm down

PUBLISHING

First published 2021 by Malcolm Down Publishing Ltd
www.malcolmdown.co.uk

24 23 22 21   7 6 5 4 3 2 1

British Library Cataloguing in Publication Data
A catalogue record for this book is available from the British Library.

ISBN 978-1-912863-75-4

Cover design by Esther Kotecha
Art direction by Sarah Grace

Printed in the UK

In Memory Of
George Elias Economou
18th June 2013 – 8th August 2020

Contents

Foreword

Reading Andy's book is a rather bizarre experience – people sometimes speak of 'a refreshing honesty' but for me the sheer depth of the articulation of deep emotional tensions and stresses is very, very challenging. I know of no-one else who really says this stuff and I admit to feeling indicted that I personally could never be so open and transparent. So, 'Beware!' – reading this work may make you decidedly uncomfortable if you have ever harboured the notion of being yourself a 'person of integrity', when deep down you know that you could never, ever reveal the secrets of your own soul as Andy does herein.

The manner in which Andy relates real-to-life encounters is both simultaneously entirely recognisable and embarrassingly cringe-worthy. The congruity with how he explains matters with one's own internal resonances is simply quite startling – he could even be using your own mind as he reveals from the inside-out some truths which, while there in us all, would never see the light of day, if left to us.

Andy's explanation of the 'unwanted' prayer at the beginning of chapter 5 is particularly excruciatingly 'difficult' – on the one hand, which self-respecting Christian would ever refuse prayer from another while simultaneously (if one did not want that particular prayer) would ever overtly refuse such benign well-wishing and risk hurting the other well-meaning soul (to see things positively) and damage one's own reputation as a kind, spiritual person – especially in the eyes on an on-looking not-yet believer? Andy leaves it to the reader to infer how he is feeling at the time and simply reflects on the other modes of brokenness which are not so visible but also in need of prayer, but ignored frequently since such needs are undercover.

Indeed, Andy's ability to explain how his sometimes-sceptical thoughts later prove accurate while also showing that he later realised he had missed something significant by building a plausible construction is again a repeated phenomenon in my own private world of thought. However, it is Andy's capacity for humility in his deep reflection and that transparency again to admit to his previously unrevealed cynicism when news of a particular suicide emerged and he had to re-calibrate his opinion on another's presumed cushy life compared to his own – which gives us pause. How many of us simply get stuff wrong like this but never admit it?

Andy's very helpful reflections here remind me of the (perhaps) clichéd old hymn 'Count Your Blessings' as he proceeds to delineate the quality of his life enriched by beautiful relationships despite his physical disability, whereas other solitary persons are imprisoned in a dark loneliness with no seeming possibility any time soon of remission.

Andy's analogy of 'Dave the Fixer of Cars' while rather quirky does get to the heart of the reputational damage we may inadvertently apply to God's name when we make extravagant claims about universal healing as a right for believers and a sometimes-blessing for non-believers: when 'healing' does not occur as promulgated so vociferously at times, to whence may one retreat? If we are embarrassed, how must God feel? Andy offers a much more nuanced approach to the consideration of the multiple facets of 'healing' properly understood.

Andy is lucid that the Gospels show Jesus as always compassionate, while silently also indicating that Jesus did not heal everyone that he could have healed, despite occasional hyperbolic language. Andy is equally clear that while faith is frequently signalled as present, with little comment on its quality or quantity, there is not given a particular formula nor any relationship indicated (always) between such faith and any eventual healing outcome.

Andy's construction on Jesus' comment in John 5, 'Stop sinning or some worse evil may befall you', which he interprets as eternal loss, is plausible, but whereas I should agree that sickness/suffering is not the inevitable corollary of sinning, I do not think one can deny that some sickness/suffering *is* a result of some sinning – in the simple idea that 'actions have consequences' kind of way, i.e. if one is promiscuous one may contract an unwelcome STD, or if one drink-drives s/he or another may be injured. I read Jesus' words in this context as just such a more immediate caution not merely some form of delayed retribution.

I really liked the thought that God redeems disability and the idea of both Jacob with his limp and Jesus with his post-resurrection scars were each bearing a badge of honour. It all depends on how one views things as to their full significance.

On prayer itself, Andy's breaking it down to three aspects of asking, seeking and knocking is well elaborated. How many Christians know the truth of what he offers here? 'You cannot force God's arm by pestering for something that is against God's will.' It seems obvious, but incorrect exegesis and hermeneutical application of the principles in several parabolic teaching have been misconstrued. Andy's commentary here is worth hearing. He challenges the reader to properly understand the deep process and purpose of prayer which is to better discern the Father's will and not simply to have a specific request met. Again, Andy's suggestion of applying his four 'ethical pillars' derived from his medical background to a general understanding of prayer, in church and out of it, really should have traction with most believers when fully understood – like those four legs on a table!

All in all, this is a most uplifting book, not least in the clear assertion that when considering either healing or hurting 'God is all over it' – despite pre-conceived assumptions as to how he ought to appear and 'perform'. Speaking from the inside-out, the veracity of Andy's own deeply personal experiences should be heard by many. Few, if any, who read this work, will be disappointed.

Liam Hanna
Director of Academic Development
Regents Theological College, Malvern

1
God's Provision

Nine years ago I had a brain stem stroke when I was just thirty-three years old. This is not a big stroke, however it is in one of the most crucial parts of the brain. It's rare to meet someone with this type of injury because if you have a stroke in such an area then it's usually fatal. The effect of the initial stroke is to stop everything that travels through the brain stem from working, leaving somebody with the ability to blink, as this is an extension of the brain, but literally nothing else, including breathing. Luckily I was already in a hospital when I lost the ability to breathe so I was quickly put on life support whilst the swelling in my brain reduced. As it did my ability to breathe independently returned but very little else. Nine years on I have a small flicker of movement in my right thumb and I can utter a few words that people who are familiar with me can understand. Physically there has been very little healing but in this book I want to talk about the healing that has taken place. I now not only have a life worth living but one I enjoy and believe one day I could be content in every circumstance.

Does that mean I'm happy with my lot? Well, not really, I'm only trying to convey that I don't live in a state of perpetual despair. I can't claim that I never harbour despairing thoughts and I wanted to give an account of how I sometimes feel.

I heard a prayer by a man about my age talking about his own feelings of desperation. He also was battling the effects of ill health, although his was a terminal illness rather than a complex disability like mine. Like me, he retained his basic belief in God but there were moments when he felt totally let down and hopeless. His words are a great reflection of how I still feel sometimes. This is what he said.

'In the very prime of life I have to leave. Whatever time I have left is spent in death's waiting room. No more glimpses of GOD in the land of the living, no more meetings with my neighbours, no more rubbing shoulders with friends. This body I inhabit is taken down and packed away like a camper's tent. Like a weaver, I've rolled up the carpet of my life as God cuts me free of the loom and at day's end sweeps up the scraps and pieces. I cry for help until morning. Like a lion, God pummels and pounds me, relentlessly finishing me off. I squawk like a doomed hen, moan like a dove. My eyes ache from looking up for help: "Master, I'm in trouble! Get me out of this!" But what's the use? God himself gave me the word. He's done it to me. I can't sleep – I'm that upset, that troubled.' (Isaiah 38:10-15 MSG)

This prayer was written by somebody about my age but it was actually written in ancient Israel nearly 3,000 years ago. Despite technologies, social media, medical advances and our various enlightenments, some things don't change.

I wrote a book in 2015 that catalogued my journey since the stroke. I had just turned thirty-three when I went to hospital with a persistent headache. I was working as a postgraduate tutor on Friday and by the Tuesday I had locked-in syndrome, unable to move anything except my eyelids. I couldn't breathe for myself, I was incontinent and in an induced coma. I spent three and a half months in an acute hospital followed by six and a half months in rehabilitation. In September 2012 I returned home and we began to have twenty-four hour 'live in' care. I began to explore how assistive technology could help me; I still had very limited physical movement but with the right technology to connect me to the world via the internet it meant that there was a huge amount I *could* do. It took a few years but now I have an incredible team taking care of me. I spoke about the closeness of my friends and family and this has only increased as the years have passed and the arrival of Samuel our miracle child. I spoke about how our holidays had been important to break up the monotony of our lives and in 2017 we used our own experiences to inform us of the best way to convert a holiday bungalow for people with additional needs. When I wrote the first book I was beginning a university degree in Theology; I have now been awarded a BA HONs in Applied Theology and I'm about to go on to study for a graduate certificate in counselling.

Towards the end of the book there were green shoots, not of physical recovery but indications that my life may still have some purpose and perhaps my stroke didn't cause the end of my usefulness to God.

The beginning of the book was quite distressing for my friends and family to read as it catalogued what it was like for me in those first few months. As I said towards the end of the book, there were green shoots indicating that God could be beginning to radically change my life but I still had enormous questions about God's purposes behind prayer and healing. I don't think it was just my decision to study Theology for six years; I think in hindsight it was a direct intention of God for me to go to Regents Theological College. Like many of the healing and other miracles discussed in this book, at the outset it seems like we may be doing something in our own strength or doing something very natural and it's only in hindsight that we see the divine hand of God.

As young Christians, we readily learn clichés like 'God allows suffering so that others can marvel at God's ability to sustain us' or 'we suffer in order to help others better deal with their own suffering'. There may be some part-truths in these platitudes about God's purpose behind suffering but I know when I'm lying motionless in my bed on my back with my arms by my sides, staring at the ceiling, unable to sleep and fearing the future, a simplistic reassurance doesn't help; there must be something more. I know that there are parts of my suffering that nobody except God and I know about so how is that bringing him any glory? Perhaps there is a greater purpose to disability than just to birth humility and compassion in an individual or to use the person with the disability to somehow showcase God's healing.

In 2014 I read a book called *God on Mute* by Pete Greig. I had already begun writing some of the chapters for my first book but there were things he said that influenced me so greatly that I actually amended my work to include a quote from him. Before commencing this publication I read another book by Pete Greig (*How to Pray: A Simple Guide for Normal People*); this was one of the catalysts to making me write again. His book was about prayer. I was a little disappointed by the release date as it was published just a few weeks after I had submitted my university dissertation on the same subject, so I was unable to use his wisdom to inform my own work.

What it did mean is that I read his book shortly after reading a number of other books about prayer and something really impacted me, giving me the surprising motivation to write again. I used to say I would only write a second book when I received my complete healing. I said this to sound really faithful but actually it was cynical and faithless. I had no intention of writing more and so making a further book dependent on receiving full healing was one way I could ensure that people didn't expect me to write again.

I do not want to share Pete's story as it's not mine to share and, moreover, he does a far better job than I could. What made his book so unique amongst books on prayer was not his testimony of miracles. The miracles he described were truly breathtaking but there were others equally incredible attested to in the other books I had read. What struck me and made me consider writing again were his experiences of unanswered prayer.

Most books about prayer offer at least one chapter to the subject of unanswered prayer but, in my experience, a lot of them read something like this: 'God doesn't always answer our prayers in the way we expect but we must remain persistent and not give up.' The books would then go on to give an example such as 'we prayed every week and God didn't answer but we didn't give up and eventually we got a breakthrough'. In essence, chapters on unanswered prayer are often chapters about prayers that aren't answered for many years but always have a positive answer eventually. Pete's book was different; his unanswered prayer was simply unanswered. He concluded that it was answered in part and he even suggested reasons why our prayers may sometimes not be fully answered in the way we expect but ultimately some of his most fervent petitions simply didn't seem to get through to God. This was just like me. I could see God working in my life and the lives of my family but there seemed to be a big black hole surrounding prayers for my physical healing. What made Pete's book so inspiring to me was not the lists of answered prayer and testimony of miracles but the fact that all of these were happening against a backdrop of very real unanswered prayer in his own life. Somehow Pete's book wouldn't have meant so much to me if his testimony was complete. It seems many testimonies are considered only worth telling when they are tied up neatly with a red bow.

Something else he said spoke to me. Everyone knows when a bush is on fire – it is burnt up by the flames – but in Exodus Moses realised God was in the bush not because it was doing anything really impressive, it was simply not being consumed by the flames. Some days Emma and I are just trying to get through the day. We want a fulfilling life and to be good parents and good friends but Pete made me understand that because our lives are in flames, all we have to do to make God's presence apparent is to prevent our situation from consuming us. This is something I want to communicate in the pages of this book. I will try to be honest about some of the flames surrounding us and give an account of the hope we still have despite the flames.

'All discipline for the moment seems not to be joyful, but sorrowful; yet to those who have been trained by it, afterwards it yields the peaceful fruit of righteousness.' (Hebrews 12:11 NASB)

I believe that God has created things such that there is a redemptive quality to suffering. Even though I don't believe God causes suffering I do believe, like gold being purified by fire, there is a beauty of character that can sometimes only be brought about in the furnace of suffering. We have the privilege of knowing many people who have proven this to be the case; through perseverance in the face of suffering they have had to exercise moral muscle that has developed beautiful character. This can be true regardless of whether someone professes faith in Christ or not. Emma and I know couples who are in a similar situation to ours and yet seem to cope without a faith in God, or at least one that they attest to. However, I know that in our life our faith and God's provision has been the only thing that could have sustained us. This sustaining power of Jesus is so common amongst Christians who are experiencing difficulties and yet we still talk more about, and hanker after, physical healing or the removal of trials. In this book I want to acknowledge that God can and does heal supernaturally but focus on and champion the ways in which God often sustains his children when he doesn't remove the trial. The Israelites understood this better than we do. The Hebrew words that are translated as heal, healing, healer or healed appear sixty-seven times in the Old Testament, however the Hebrew word that refers to being sustained appears 1,306 times.

When the Israelites were in the desert they were praying for the promised land and for forty years God didn't give it to them. Instead he sustained them where they were. He did incredible miracles providing manna and quail to help sustain them during that long time in the wilderness. They must have wondered why he didn't just deliver them. Moreover, they were unable to stockpile the provision meaning that they had to rely on God every day to sustain them for the next twenty-four hours.

The prayer I mentioned earlier was written by King Hezekiah and recorded in the book of Isaiah. He was so ill that Isaiah actually visited him with a message from God that he should get his affairs in order because he was going to die. King Hezekiah prayed to God and asked for healing. To all intents and purposes God granted the healing but his choice of words emphasised what actually happened. God said I will add fifteen years to your life. From an eternal perspective our bodies are all terminally ill. They do wear out and they will die, sometimes it's after seventy or eighty years and other times it's less than that. When King Hezekiah prayed, God said he would sustain him for a further fifteen years but although his body became well again it was still in the state of decline that all life on earth experiences. Even if our bodies experience healing it's only partial in that they will die after a few more years. The only true healing happens after death when we are given a fully restored body.

I want this book to help people to understand the potential harm the church can inadvertently cause to people who are suffering by only teaching about God's desire to heal and neglecting the wish that he may want to provide and sustain.

I am not there yet but I know Paul said he found contentment in all situations and that is my hope. This is how the prayer I shared earlier in the chapter concludes:

'O Master, these are the conditions in which people live, and yes, in these very conditions my spirit is still alive - fully recovered with a fresh infusion of life! It seems it was good for me to go through all those troubles. Throughout them all you held tight to my lifeline. You never let me tumble over the edge into nothing. But my sins you let go of, threw them over your shoulder - good riddance! The dead don't thank you and choirs don't sing praises from the morgue. Those buried six feet under don't witness to your faithful ways. It's the living - live men, live women - who thank you, just as I'm doing right now. Parents give their children full reports on your faithful ways. God saves and will save me. As fiddles and mandolins strike up the tunes, we'll sing, oh we'll sing, sing, for the rest of our lives in the Sanctuary of God.' (Isaiah 38:16-20 MSG)

2
The Good, The Bad and The Ugly

Emma and I continued attending the same church in Selly Oak, Birmingham, that I have been attending for seventeen years. My friend Pastor Stuart, who was the church leader in the first book, contacted me on Facebook in 2016 and asked if he could come round and talk to me that week. This was ominous because if Stuart wanted to ask me anything, he would just drop me a message and if he wanted to speak to me in person, I saw him every week. He came round and Emma offered him a drink. He quickly got down to the reason for his visit.

'Elim Church headquarters have made a new position with me in mind and asked if I would consider leaving CLC and becoming the new Director of Ministry for Elim.'

I was shocked. It wasn't a surprise that the people at Elim had recognised Stuart's incredible talent and opted to put it to use, but I couldn't believe he was leaving! We talked about his new responsibilities; what would his family do? And who would ever replace him at CLC? The reason Stuart had wanted to see me this week in particular was because he wanted to tell certain people in person before he announced it in church in a few days' time. I was intensely saddened at the news but because of my stroke, my reaction was still over the top and I sobbed. I explained that I thought it might be wise if I didn't come to church on Sunday when he announced it as my emotional reaction may be inappropriate. Stuart said he quite liked the idea of announcing his departure to sounds of sobbing coming from the back of the church, but I pointed out that my emotions were quite unpredictable and he could just as easily be sharing his sad news to sounds of cackling laughter, which wouldn't be quite so edifying. Stuart agreed it might be best if I wasn't there. The church is now led by Andy and it's been rebranded as Christian Life Church. A number of the congregation left in the months following Stuart's departure which made his departure even harder. Many of the people who had been my friends for many years – and knew me before my stroke – left. With their departure came many new Christians to the church but although everyone still knew who I was, I felt like they only saw who I was now and not who I used to be.

In late 2019 I was finding it more of a challenge at church. Emma was leading the creche upstairs so I was often on my own in the auditorium. Dozens of people would stop and talk to me but I was unable to talk back; there was also no space to socialise so I would often leave during the last song. It meant I was attending church most weeks but I was missing out on so much fellowship. I went with my carer to try out a few churches in Bournville that I could travel to myself in my wheelchair. One week, when Emma was available to come with me, we visited a church that meets in a secondary school just yards from our house. The visit got off to a good start: as I approached the front door it automatically opened and I was able to drive straight in. This may sound very trivial but after years of waiting for people to open the double doors especially for me, this seemed like a real provision. Straightaway Emma recognised people that she knew from the church in which she grew up. Next, the senior pastor introduced himself and we got talking about some of the struggles associated with a complex disability as he has a son with complex needs. Emma and I felt immediately welcome and because the church met in a large school building there was lots of space to mix after the service and talk. We felt at home. As if God was confirming that this was the right church, a woman came up to me and said, 'Are you Andy?'

'Yes,' I replied.

She then introduced herself as Anne, the person I had been emailing. When I was planning to write this book, a friend of a friend suggested somebody called Anne who lived in my area and might be willing to help. It turned out Anne had been attending that church for about eighteen years, she had a degree in Theology and an interest in childhood disability. She had been sat in church on the day we visited and, having seen me, felt prompted to introduce herself as she was fairly confident I was the person who had been exchanging emails with her for a few weeks. Next, another lady came up to me and introduced herself as the person I had been talking to over the last few weeks about disabled holidays. I didn't even realise she was from Birmingham let alone attending this church. Soon after, we had a meeting with our old senior pastor to thank him for all the support the church had given over the years and to express that we were not leaving because we were unhappy but rather we felt we were being called somewhere else. We had already decided to move churches but things continued to fall into place, giving Emma and me even more certainty we had made the right decision. Since my stroke I hadn't been consciously aware that I was missing being part of a home group. I had long since accepted that most people don't have accessible homes so, unless we hosted a small home group ourselves, we were unlikely to ever be invited. We found out the senior pastor and his wife hosted a small community group and because their home was adapted with their son in mind it meant I could attend. It was such a special night, so normal, yet I hadn't been to a small fellowship group in someone's home for over nine years. Emma was also excited to learn that there was a monthly meeting set up to enable individuals who cared for somebody to socialise and it has since been a lifeline to Emma.

I have quite rightly attributed my recovery to God but for many years I only knew God was there because of the love of Emma and my church family. Ultimately God can provide for all our needs but he often does this through his church, so I believe faith in God without the fellowship of a church community is limited.

Church therefore is vital for anyone who needs God's provision; however, there are times when church can actually hurt a bit so it's vital that we as the church recognise this and strive to avoid some of these hurts that we may inadvertently cause.

I was sitting in my wheelchair slumped forward and, with every bump in the road, the muscles of my lower back stretched and strained. There weren't any tears anymore; they had stopped about ten minutes earlier and now I was just numb. The weather outside was cold and wet and the standing water on the road was splattering the undercarriage of my wheelchair-accessible vehicle and making a deafening road noise. I couldn't see where we were because my head was just looking at my feet but I could see the pulsing orange glow from the sodium street lights illuminating the cabin as we passed them. David, Emma's dad, was driving and we seemed to be heading towards Bournville. This was strange because David's car was at his home (we had picked him up in the morning) but now I think Emma and her dad just wanted to get me home. I went straight to bed still feeling numb and Emma folded down her mattress on the floor of our former dining room, not wanting me to sleep alone, whilst David rang a taxi to get him back to his house seven or eight miles away. I lay on my back as I always do and replayed the evening in my mind. I didn't want to talk or pray but just wanted to try and make sense of what I'd witnessed.

About a year after my stroke we got news of a healing crusade coming to Birmingham and with excitement predicted this may be the vehicle God was to use to either do a complete miraculous healing or perhaps act as the catalyst for a more gradual one. Either way, whether I received healing myself or not, witnessing God's power in action would surely give a much-needed boost to my faith and I was excited. We wanted to go for the whole day so we drove over to Emma's parents and picked up her dad to act as both company and support for Emma and myself. Throughout the day there were a number of distinguished speakers. These were not stereotypical health and prosperity preachers with an apparent self-serving theology to generate wealth, but missionaries who genuinely cared and were bringing in a great harvest of souls along with a credible healing ministry. There were a number of speakers sharing stories about the incredible works God had done in their lives and those of people they knew. The entire day seemed to be building to a crescendo. The final meeting would be a meeting for specific prayer for healing, and expectation was growing.

Finally 7.30 p.m. arrived and it was the beginning of the final meeting, which was going to be a crusade to pray for healing. Expectation had already been made that tonight was the night God was going to do something pretty fantastic. The main speaker gave his thoughts about the nature of God and his interpretation of God's expectations of us; this was all backed up with anecdotes of great miracles and we were told God was going to prove his word in just a few minutes with signs and wonders. As the entire auditorium began to pray there was almost a frenzy of expectation swirling around amongst the audience, and as the speaker counted down from three, the suspense was almost unbearable. After the prayer we said 'Amen' and the speaker announced how powerful he had felt the presence of God. I hadn't felt anything but perhaps that was just a reflection of the dearth of my own faith. They asked people to give testimony to healing that they had just received and I looked around – hundreds of people were beginning to queue up to go onto the stage and do just that. They genuinely seemed excited.

At first people seemed to be giving thanks to God for easing cold symptoms or that of acute tiredness. There were testimonies of people with stiff limbs that had become looser and people kept coming and coming to bring their thanks and gratitude for these works God had done. Crucially no-one from the wheelchair section joined the queue and just watched on as the speaker got ever more excited about the 'proof' of God's power that had been demonstrated. I watched on in quiet numbness not really knowing how to process what I was seeing. I didn't want to dismiss any of these reported healings but I couldn't silence the voice at the back of my mind saying, 'For goodness' sake, what is this about?' I'm sure if I had voiced my concern, those around me and probably myself would have just said, 'That's the devil taunting you; you must have faith,' but I could only look on with ever more cynicism as I heard about God releasing people from their sniffs and snuffles.

I don't really remember how the meeting ended but we slowly wheeled out in silence. Before I exited the auditorium two of my friends, who had been sat in the stands behind me, rushed to pray for me; this wasn't a 'prayer of power' petitioning God for a miraculous provision but a quiet prayer that my soul would be settled and that my faith would be preserved. Seeing my friends seemed to break the stunned trance I was in and a feeling of ache and despair started to well up. I was desperate to get back to my car as soon as possible but when we arrived at the carpark somebody had parked their own wheelchair vehicle across the entrance so that no-one could get past and we had to sit in the rain watching them slowly enter and be secured in their vehicle before we could even approach ours. Soaking wet I was wheeled up the ramp and my heart finally broke. I had kept my composure for so long but now it was like a dam being removed and the emotion of not just that day but months of suppressed feelings began to flood out. In the early days after my stroke I often got upset but for some time now I had remained emotionally stable. But now was different. I let out bellows of sobs and the feeling of despair felt like it would kill me. I half expected Emma and her dad to try and comfort me but I think they knew exactly what I was thinking and they didn't have any more answers than me.

The next morning I woke up early. I was calm, maybe resigned, but I kept replaying the excitement the evangelist had shown in response to what seemed to me like very trivial healings. I couldn't get my head around what would cause someone who regularly saw the lame walking, the blind seeing or the deaf hearing to get so excited about someone who could now lift their arm ten degrees higher. Over the next few days I continued to be haunted by my memories of that night and various friends and pastoral leaders tried to give me a new perspective to work with. In time the feelings softened but they never really went away. I decided whatever the rights or wrongs of such meetings were, they were not right for me. I found it so hard making a decision to avoid them because this seemed to just confirm the idea of my fickle faith, but that crusade had caused weeks of hurt, confusion and depression and I didn't think there had been any harvest of fruit in my life as a result.

A few months later Emma and I were at a conference and one of the sessions was about healing, 'Perhaps this could shed a little bit of light about God's intentions.' After just a few minutes, to my horror I realised we had inadvertently attended a practical session for healing and, once again, I seemed to be 'the fattened calf' in the room just waiting to be served up. We sat through wave after wave of what felt like veiled criticism for my predicament, the usual suspects with the stiff knee and acute weariness gave thanks as God released his healing power upon them but once again there wasn't so much as a splash coming my way. I could feel myself getting upset but I was trapped: if I left halfway through, everyone would see me and assume the speaker had touched a nerve about the sin lingering in my life; but if I stayed I knew I would cry, which I was unable to stifle. I signalled to Emma we had to go and I just managed to maintain my composure until the seminar room door closed behind me and I crumbled in the corridor outside. I was consumed by guilt for my own cynicism and I knew I couldn't have faith whilst still feeling things sometimes resembled a pantomime. But what could I do? I could choose what I did despite my feelings, but I couldn't actually change what I felt.

This experience led me to avoid any meeting when the title of the event included the word 'healing'. This was an awful thing as surely I needed God's healing as much as anyone but I had to consider my emotional health as well as my physical health, and I knew there was a risk that such an event may cause more harm to the former.

Both of these experiences happened within eighteen months of my stroke and really impacted me. I have been a Christian for as long as I can remember and prior to my stroke I was involved in leadership, yet these experiences still really harmed my faith. It made me think what would it do to an immature Christian or a non-Christian attending with a friend? Six months later I began a six-year part-time Theology degree with the hope that I would never be so shaken by that sort of event ever again.

A retired pastor once said to me one of his greatest worries was what people in his church might say about God that he didn't believe. He said that he just had to accept that not everything everybody said was necessarily what he believed himself. Once Emma and I were at church one evening for a special guest speaker. Because it was somebody different, people had been told to invite friends who didn't normally go to church. I was sat in my usual position, which is relatively close to the entrance so most people do see me when they arrive. After the service, a man and his wife came to speak to Emma about me. I was there too, but they were not speaking to me but about me. That man looked quite official and, had I not been a member of the church for a number of years, I would have believed that they had some special position of responsibility. They asked Emma if we had been praying for healing and when Emma explained we had in the past but now we tended to pray about smaller goals, they explained the continuance of my disability and the apparent failure of prayer was a result of un-forgiveness on my part and we should therefore reach out, repent and then our prayers would be more effective. Emma rarely gets agitated in public and was still a lot more civil than most people would have been in that situation, but she told them firmly that was not what we believed and their words could be quite offensive. I was quite happy being defended so fervently by Emma and my own theology on the matter meant that the words of a stranger were not going to upset me. I then had a comforting thought.

Before my stroke, I had a number of responsibilities in the church, but since I had become unwell I was unable to do any of them and I often joked the only thing I was good for in church was to be a very elaborate doorstop. I don't know if it was a picture from God, but I started thinking about the blue lights that you get in some butchers or bakeries: there is normally an intense blue light in a box that hangs on the wall. The light is so attractive to flies that they ignore the raw meat or the pastries and fly towards the light. When they get close to the light, they don't see the thin wires carrying an electric current and let's just say they're neutralised. I thought about myself in my wheelchair being like one of those lights. In my experience, there are often some Christians who just cannot help but be attracted to the person they perceive is most in need of their ministry, like the light in the butchers. Those people are so attracted to me that they are not able to hurt other people with their black-and-white thinking, Bible passages taken out of context and lack of tact or grace. I was effectively neutralising their hurtful comments. When I shared this story with my brother he commented, 'Is Emma the electric wire?' By attempting to re-educate me about God's intentions for my life, it was neutralising what they thought. I was quite happy to let them witter on, telling me what I must do, and it actually gave me a buzz to see the church slowly emptying whilst I was keeping the rest of the unsuspecting congregation safe from false doctrines.

If these doctrines and the sort of events I described earlier are prevalent in churches today, where have we gone wrong? Would I really want to encourage a non-Christian disabled friend to subject themselves to that? The wider church family have been invaluable to Emma and myself since the stroke and I have often commented I don't know how I would have coped without a faith and the church. Overwhelmingly, the church has had a really positive effect since my stroke but it has been punctuated by a few very negative experiences such as those I have just described. They are so rare they are barely significant; however, if someone's first few experiences of Christianity included such an experience, would they ever stick around to receive the massive support that both faith in God and the church family can bring?

In the next chapter I want to consider a few of the different approaches to healing that are prevalent in the church. Rather than making a judgement about which I believe are doctrinally sound and which are open to interpretation, I want to consider how the different approaches might affect a disabled person.

3
Approaches to Healing

During my first two years at university I was getting reasonable marks for my essays but my performance in exams was barely satisfactory, and sometimes I only passed the year by managing to compensate my poor examination mark with a better essay mark. So for my third year I knew things had to change. Before my stroke I used to enjoy exams but since starting Bible college these were by far my weakest discipline. I have a more scientific mind so I would feel much more comfortable writing a list of relevant bullet points in contrast to the descriptive waffle that I perceived was expected for an arts degree. Moreover, as a result of my stroke my eyes were unable to focus on text so any revision had to be done with my study facilitator. However, even this still left me unable to visualise how it was written down on the page, making it harder than ever to remember during exams.

At the beginning of my third year I decided to make a new plan. I would look at a few key subjects that were likely to come up in the exam, and really major on revising for these. I would then just adapt what I had learned to make it relevant to the specific question being asked. Before my exam I had intensely revised a number of subjects which could come up so I was just looking forward to seeing which ones I could use.

On the morning of the exam I set up my recliner in our church in order to be able to lie back and dictate my answers. I had previously written my exams at college but my main personal assistant was away so the college allowed me to do my exam closer to home with Stuart, our senior pastor, invigilating. There were about twelve different questions and I had to choose three of them: one about church history, one about the Bible and a third about the practicalities of ministry. The question I chose for this final section was about a friend recently diagnosed with a serious illness. I was asked what pastoral advice I would give to him. This seemed like the sort of question for which God had been training me for the last four and a half years, but I wanted to stick to my plan of regurgitating a rehearsed answer, so I started my answer a bit like this:

'The first thing I would want to tell my friend about would be the six different approaches to healing that are prevalent in the church today.'

I then proceeded to dictate my planned answer about the six approaches to healing. When I started to speak I could see Rachel, my study facilitator, trying to stifle her grin. She had been present for all my revision and knew exactly what I was doing. After I had finished shoe-horning this well-revised bit of information into my answer, we packed up and went home. Over the next few hours and days I reflected upon this question and composed in my head what I would actually say to my friend that might possibly give some comfort. Surely I should be able to give some special counsel that would make a difference. I had been given a huge amount of advice myself so I knew first-hand what was and was not helpful. The more I considered what my true response would be, I increasingly felt that although this may not have been the first thing I would have talked about, I would have in time wanted to give some background to my friend about the different approaches Christians might advocate for securing God's healing. Perhaps the exam answer I wrote wasn't so misplaced after all.

I had experienced all sorts of claims and counter claims about why I was ill and what I needed to do to get better and although I felt peace about some of these and uneasiness about others, it would have been reassuring to have at my fingertips the theology behind those theories to help me understand where people were coming from.

The methods I had learned were described by Ronald A.N. Kydd in a book called *Healing Through the Centuries*. This was particularly good because Kydd didn't try to advocate one approach over another. He just explained what they were and why people believed them. This allowed me to add my own thoughts and criticisms of the different approaches and specifically consider how they might be perceived by a suffering individual. Some of the approaches are more prevalent in particular denominations.

The first method he described he called *Confrontational*. This approach to healing suggests that illness is due to demonic forces and there is an emphasis on illness being caused by these demons. By using the authority given to Christians by Jesus, the demons can be exorcised and the person healed. This was a particularly prevalent approach to healing in the early 20th century, however it's still popular amongst some churches today. Although I wouldn't want to dismiss the possibility of a demonic cause for some illnesses, I would counsel my friend that people may only naively suggest it because it was prevalent in the culture they grew up in and not because of any specific knowledge from God. I think it's a very dangerous thing to suggest unless you can be certain, as you could leave the suffering individual searching for what they could possibly have done to allow this demon to affect them in such a way. If in a very rare situation there was a demonic element to the suffering, it should be dealt with by church friends and family, and not as a spectacle for entertainment.

When I woke up from my coma I remember having a Catholic medallion on a chain by my bed. It was a St Christopher. There was a legend about St Christopher carrying Christ as a child across a river and for centuries people have prayed to St Christopher for protection, especially on journeys. Obviously in my situation someone thought it would be beneficial to ask St Christopher to intercede on my behalf as they believed he had a special relationship with God and therefore his influence might be beneficial. This was an example of Kydd's second approach: *Intercessory*. This suggested there were specific people or saints we could pray to and they would intercede for us. Other Christians believe that when Christ died he removed that separation between us and God and now the Holy Spirit can intercede directly on our behalf. Generally I would agree with them, however that medallion was very precious to me as it came to represent all the Catholic people who were praying for me and my family. The medallion was only symbolic for me in reminding me that there were hundreds of people praying for me even though they didn't necessarily share every nuance of doctrine that I believed.

Kydd's third approach was called *Reliquarial*. This conjured up images of the daring Indiana Jones searching for ancient objects or bones belonging to holy people, which supposedly had magical powers. Although in some Orthodox churches these holy relics are revered, Kydd's approach also referred to God's power being transmitted through any inanimate object. In the Bible, in Acts 19, the apostle Paul prayed over handkerchiefs which were given to the sick who were unable to come in person. When I was first ill I had a prayer handkerchief tucked inside my pyjama top. Emma's parents' church had a huge prayer meeting especially for healing every week and they would also pray over handkerchiefs which could be given to people unable to attend. On the face of it, an inanimate object possessing some sort of healing power does not fit with my beliefs in general. However, when I became aware of its presence it began to mean something similar to the Catholic St Christopher medallion. It was a tangible way of remembering that I was in the prayers of hundreds of people.

The first three approaches to healing I have described all suggest that healing might be instantaneous and a miraculous event, but the fourth approach suggested something a bit different. It suggested that divine healing didn't have to be instantaneous but God could bring his healing power over time. This was known as an *Incubational* model. In the early 20th century there were healing homes. These were places where people could go and stay for a few months and gradually over that time, with prayer, they would become well. Today some Christian drug rehabilitation centres are similar in that they take a very broken person with life-controlling addictions and slowly, through prayer and community, God restores them. For me, the healing home was my own home, being surrounded by the love of friends and family. Although it didn't have dramatic effects on my physical health, over time, my mental health was restored from a very tortured place, to one of peace.

Kydd describes his fifth approach as *Revelational*. In my experience this has often left me feeling guilty for the scepticism that I cannot help feeling. I feel guilty because I don't doubt that God can reveal through prophecies, and Paul even encourages us to seek prophecies, but there is always a nagging feeling that I don't know if when I experience people claiming to have a prophecy they are being genuine or not. If prophecy builds faith then realising that you have been duped by someone who has faked a prophecy is even more destructive. It does seem to lend itself to a degree of showmanship deliberate or otherwise. This often reminds me about a large audience going to see a staged show with a medium. The performer might say, 'I'm hearing the name John might be relevant, who is it relevant to?' In a show such as this there is bound to be somebody called John or somebody related to John and so the performer knows that he's going to get a positive response. Similarly in a large healing meeting, if the preacher suggests God wants to heal somebody's back, it doesn't require a special revelation from God to predict that somebody in a crowd of four or five hundred people might have some back pain. I am confident the Holy Spirit can and does reveal prophecies about people he wishes to heal but this approach can easily be misused to manipulate an audience or individual. This may sound cynical but I think the smaller the crowd and the more specific the revelation, the more likely this has genuinely been revealed by God.

Finally we come to Kydd's sixth approach: *Soteriological*. Soteriological simply means the doctrine of salvation. Our salvation was made possible by Jesus' death on the cross which paid the price for all our sins and bought our salvation. This is not controversial amongst Christians but because ultimately we believe sickness, including disability, is a result of sin entering the world. If sins have been paid for should their effects also be eliminated? I would want to be really explicit to my friend that his DISABILITY, SICKNESS AND SUFFERING IS NOT NECESSARILY CAUSED BY ANY PERSONAL SIN ON HIS PART OR HIS ANCESTORS. However, sickness was never God's original plan. Actually, I could concede that the claim of many health and prosperity teachers that 'God wants you well' is probably true. God obviously doesn't get any pleasure from seeing our suffering but since sin entered the world this became a reality and God may now be using this terrible consequence to his advantage.

Others may tell my friend that if Jesus' atonement was sufficient for the forgiveness of his sins then it should also be sufficient for his healing. They would argue increasing somebody's faith that their healing has already been paid for can itself be the vehicle for healing to occur.

When I first read about this classification of healing into Kydd's six approaches it really helped to order in my own mind where people were coming from when they made certain suggestions. There were some approaches that I didn't necessarily think made healing more likely but it still acted as a real boost to my faith to know that people genuinely cared. I may not necessarily believe these approaches influence God's will, but in my encounters with them they caused me no hurt or distress.

I suppose in some instances people may request money in return for a product or service that they claim will help to heal, but this was never my experience. Some of the other approaches did contain elements of truth; for example we know that in some circumstances the spiritual world affects the natural or that God may be revealing his purposes to an individual as a prophecy. In these circumstances a confrontational or revelational approach could be hugely effective, however embarking on these approaches without specific knowledge from God can be very hurtful. One of the hardest doctrines I have had to come to terms with is that our lack of faith is to blame for God not acting. Even by suggesting this may not be the case, you are by definition expressing your own lack of faith and therefore confirming to the person that if you just believed like they do you would be well.

Although these are six approaches to healing that may be the ones most prevalent in the church as a whole today, should divine healing be the church's only response to disability? To eradicate it? To treat it as something so destructive that there cannot possibly be any redeeming reason for God to allow it to remain? Do individuals know that by only praying for healing and not other needs for disabled people, this may make us feel so useless to God that his only possible way of using our life again is if he first conforms us to other people's expectations of what a 'normal' blessed Christian should look like?

In the next chapter I want to suggest that everybody has limitations and whereas some are visible or diagnosable, others are considered personality traits or consequences of place of birth or upbringing. Are the limitations we can see or diagnose the most important to be eradicated?

4
WHO Most Needs Healing?

Once I was visiting a church with my carer. I didn't normally require my carer to be there but it was certainly easier while Samuel was so young to have an extra pair of hands. She had expressed a desire to be able to help and also to see the church that we had been so positive about. As always the atmosphere was wonderful and the presence of God was tangible and I was proud to be a Christian. The worship, preaching and community were witnessing on my behalf to my carer as well as fulfilling my own spiritual needs. At the end of the service a few people, who we knew, came over to say hello and introduce themselves to my carer. Others who we hadn't met before were just welcoming us and the whole experience was great.

As we were wheeling out, a man stopped us to introduce himself and welcome us which was wonderful. However, he then did something that made me cringe. He reached out, put his hand on my head and began praying. What for? He didn't know what my needs were. He could assume I didn't particularly like being in a wheelchair but was he just assuming I wanted prayer for that? My carer felt even more awkward. Her job, amongst other things, was to protect me, and a total stranger reaching out and resting his hand on my head was something she didn't know if she should stop or not. As it happens I've been in churches for many years and despite me thinking certain things are perhaps inappropriate, I do not normally feel upset or threatened by people behaving like this. Although on this occasion I was a bit embarrassed and offended that out of the hundreds of people in that room, many of whom were in desperate need of God's provision, this man scanned the room and saw me as the most needy. I imagine in a crowd of people that big there would have been failing marriages, abusive relationships, hidden addictions or worse, but because they weren't visible all his attention was on my perceived needs.

This situation caused me to reflect about my varying needs. Some needs are on display for all to see but I also have those that nobody except God knows about. Moreover, some people who appear to have no obvious limitation have issues so great that they dwarf all of mine.

Society understands mental health so much better now, but it still seems unimaginable that I could be content whilst living with a catastrophic disability, whereas a physically well person could be so disillusioned with life that they no longer want to live.

A few months ago, I was looking for a new personal care assistant. I had been on the website that I normally use but I had no success. A friend recommended someone to me who she had met and already did the type of work I needed. We exchanged emails and he agreed to come and work with me. I sent him the employee starter forms to sign, but five days later he emailed back with another question about the job. I was able to reassure him but said I needed the forms back as soon as possible. It was another three or four days before he replied again, still expressing his desire to work for me but asking more questions. I have been employing personal care assistants for long enough to recognise when somebody is going to let me down, so I said nothing to him but ensured that somebody else was able to cover his shift. Sure enough, three days later the inevitable email arrived saying that there had been an unexpected family emergency, and he wouldn't be able to attend after all. He may not have expected the family emergency, but I had! I said nothing, but inside I was quite annoyed. Here I was with a devastating disability and I pictured him living life to the full, picking and choosing what work was most convenient for him and paying little or no regard for the people he should be caring for. A few months later, our mutual friend posted a tribute to him on social media as he had committed suicide the night before. I was a bit choked. I hadn't had many dealings with this man but the picture I had allowed to build in my mind was of a fit, athletic, fun-loving male with oodles of confidence and the ability to pick and choose what work suited his lifestyle the best. This was obviously not the reality. This tragedy made me wonder what people tell themselves about my life from what they see?

Last summer I was in the park with Emma and Samuel who was playing in a huge sand pit. After an hour or so I was getting a bit bored but Samuel was still loving it so I decided to drive my wheelchair a quarter of a mile back to our home without supervision. I was only a few hundred yards away from the park when I drove a little bit too close to a hedge. A stray branch got caught around my main power lead and pulled out the plug. My wheelchair immediately stopped. Now I was in a pickle! I can change the modes on my wheelchair and steer it side to side using only my head but if there is no power I'm stranded. I knew exactly what had happened but how would I ever be able to explain to a stranger? I quickly accepted I was going to be there for some time! It was a warm day and the sun was getting hotter. I could feel my skin beginning to burn but I couldn't do anything until Emma decided to come home and rescue me. A couple of passers-by stopped and asked if they could help but when they realised I couldn't coherently speak, they left me. After about 20 minutes, a young man came over and asked if he could help. I mumbled, 'I don't think so', and to my amazement he repeated those words back to me, before asking, 'Can I call anyone for you?' A glimmer of hope began to shine and I said, 'My wife.' He then repeated, 'You want me to call your wife?' I said 'yes' and then slowly I was able to give her number one numeral at a time until he was able to ring and speak directly to her. She quickly came and plugged my power back in and, within half an hour of the initial problem, I was moving again.

I now have a device that I wear around my neck, which has a switch I can press with my chin to send Emma a text message saying HELP ME. It also provides Emma with a link to Google maps pinpointing my exact location. It means that my physical disability can be mitigated to a large extent by this piece of technology so whereas my disability may have included the inability to go out independently, it is now no longer dangerous. A person with agoraphobia, for example, may look okay but their inability to go out independently is not so easily resolved. Similarly, although I cannot visit many of my friends as their houses are simply not accessible, unlike a person who doesn't have friends, my friends can – and do – come and see me. Being disabled is a huge struggle. It puts additional pressure on my relationships and especially my marriage, but I consider myself so fortunate to have those relationships in the first place. I personally feel for me that life without friends or a spouse may actually be more difficult than the disability.

We can see that everybody has limitations of one sort or another. This could be a mental illness or something like social awkwardness. In my case it is a physical disability which impairs the things that I could otherwise do. The limitations other people face could be poverty, abusive childhood, lack of education or health care or even a serious character flaw. We wouldn't necessarily see social awkwardness as something as serious as a physical disability but if it resulted in struggling to make or maintain relationships, I would argue the physical disability may actually be more tolerable. I may be locked in my body but the body is surrounded by dozens of relationships that are valuable to me, not least Emma. Being able to move my body but living alone with few friends would be unbearable for me.

I've only addressed about how people might view different limitations but I haven't begun to talk about how God can reveal himself through struggles. Therefore, we as the church should never compare our limitations and place them in a hierarchy of seriousness like society may do. A limitation that seems innocuous to most people could be devastating for someone else; and a disability that seems unbearable, by God's grace, can lead to just a different but equally content life.

The purpose of this chapter was to challenge the idea that there are disabled people and 'normal' people. Instead there are just people who have different limitations and need God's provision to either heal or sustain. Indeed, the gospel would suggest that our biggest need is to be in relationship with God regardless of our limitations. Next I want to look at how God addresses these fragilities whether they are visible or not and answer the question: do we still recognise God's hand in a largely secular society, where the supernatural is rarely seen? Even when something happens that could be supernatural, often a plausible scientific cause is considered a more mature or educated one.

5
HOW Does God Heal?

When I was first unwell I used to have nightmares where I was always trapped or being held down. Many times I couldn't be heard and the dreams seemed to go on for hours. I guess it's not surprising given the trauma that I was experiencing during my waking hours. Nowadays I am sometimes aware of dreaming but they are normally pleasant dreams, sometimes I am completely able-bodied but even when I am disabled in my dreams it's never as bad as reality. So I may be able to talk or my limbs will be significantly stronger, sometimes I can even walk. I would love to believe that this was a prophetic dream to encourage me that I'm going to get better. I don't know about that but I do think it gives an insight into how I view my own disability. When I have excellent care provision, the love of friends and family and the correct equipment and technology, I do not feel as disabled as I look. There are exceptions.

Last summer I was holidaying with friends and my young family, and we planned a day trip. Using my technology I had bought tickets for the aquarium and booked a table at a local restaurant. We arrived to the town mid-morning but already there were limited parking spaces. We found a long stretch of disabled parking bays at the side of the road so we pulled up and unloaded the car. My wheelchair comes out of the car on a ramp at the rear the same as most disabled vehicles but there wasn't a convenient dropped kerb. Emma and my carer walked in opposite directions to find the nearest place that I could access the wide pavement going into the town. After two or three minutes and scanning the pavement up and down the road we realised there were no dropped kerbs anywhere. These were dedicated disabled bays and yet a wheelchair couldn't get out of the road and onto the pavement anywhere. We had to pack up the car and travel to the nearest dropped kerb (about a quarter of a mile) and park again in a standard parking space. Now I felt disabled.

I have heard some wheelchair users suggest that they are not disabled, it's the world that is making them disabled. I even heard a blind man who was blind from birth say that when he is travelling round a familiar town centre that has been properly designed with his needs in mind, along with his guide dog, he feels that he actually doesn't need his sight. I think to some extent I realise that I do have significant needs, however the degree to which I feel helpless can be massively mitigated by my environment.

Nowadays we may choose to call it equality with disability awareness or proper disability planning but 2,000 years ago the writer of Hebrews called it 'making level paths'.

'"Make level paths for your feet," so that the lame may not be disabled, but rather healed.' (Hebrews 12:13)

The first way in which God heals people with disabilities is by encouraging those who aren't disabled to make the world less disabling, meaning that those who are disabled will be healed.

Next I want to share a really well-known story that many Christians will have heard before. This is a familiar story but it helps us recognise some of the other ways in which God works.

The river had burst its banks but the rain kept falling. Usually, the little stream wound its way through the picturesque village but now there was a raging torrent and there wasn't daylight visible under the bridges as the water squeezed through. The man climbed up onto the roof of his little brick shed and started praying. Cars were beginning to float away but he saw his neighbour coming to grab a few of his belongings in a tractor that he had commandeered from somewhere. He shouted to the man on the roof, 'The river is rising, why don't you get onto the tractor now before it gets worse? We can pick up some of your belongings too.'

'I'm ok,' shouted the man over the deafening roar of the water, 'I've been praying and I am confident God will save me.'

His neighbour looked sceptical but drove back to his brother's house higher up the valley. The water continued to rise but the man was not deterred, he prayed even more earnestly. Next, the man saw an inflatable dingy, the sort that lifeguards usually use, coming up the street. He thought it strange and so out of place to see such a boat in the normally quiet village. It kept stopping at different properties as the men on board were checking that there was nobody left in the buildings. One of the crew spotted him perched on his roof and shouted, 'What are you still doing here? Get into the boat and we will take you to dry land.'

The man thanked them for their concern but said, 'I'm ok, I'm just waiting for God to save me.' He then knelt back down in the water, his arms stretched up to heaven. A couple of hours later, there was a deafening noise above him and the man looked up expecting to see a miraculous provision but instead it was just a rescue helicopter that had joined the search for stranded individuals. The man sighed, bowed his head and continued praying. A voice came from the helicopter, 'We are going to hoist you.'

The man started waving his arms, 'No, no! I don't want you to hoist me, I've been praying and God is going to do a miracle. Just wait and see.'

Later that evening, the man is in heaven and he says to God, 'I don't understand why you left me to drown and didn't save me.'

God answers, 'I sent you a tractor, then a dinghy and even a helicopter, what more did you want me to do?'

There are accounts in the Bible of interventions so supernatural that they couldn't possibly have any other explanation but it would seem that the vast majority of interventions that God makes today, even when they seem quite miraculous, could technically happen by chance. There are natural physical laws in this world that God very rarely interferes with, so we can be confident that if a person jumps out of a building, they will fall accelerating at exactly 9.8 metres per second squared until they reach terminal velocity or hit the ground. Let's take this law of nature and give it a scenario. Suppose Joe has been feeling suicidal but his mum has been praying for him. His impulses overwhelm him and he climbs a high-rise building from which to jump. In this instance, believing that God could answer his mum's prayer to save Joe, doesn't mean believing that he would have to fall differently to the law of nature or even fly away. Perhaps God's divine provision would actually be a jammed window, an incredibly timed telephone call at just the right moment or even a coincidentally placed window-cleaning platform.

A lot of God's healing provision is built into our DNA, so often when we get a cut or a cold our body simply heals itself. We attribute it to our immune system but who made the immune system? When our body is unable to repair itself there is a huge base of medical knowledge so certain drugs and procedures are very effective at healing certain diseases. But where does that knowledge come from? Limiting God's healing to only the supernatural healing neglects a huge swathe of the healing God provides. I've heard it said that when we pray we should expect a miracle. This sounds like an oxymoron; the dictionary describes a miracle as something very unexpected so as soon as we expect it, it ceases to be a miracle.

I was taught a prayer many years ago that took account of this. 'I look forward in anticipation to how you will rectify this situation for your purpose.' This asserts the expectation that God is going to do something divine but doesn't attempt to suggest what that should be.

In my experience, when we pray, coincidences keep happening. I believe physiotherapy alone is not going to suddenly make me better after nine years; however, alongside prayer, the physiotherapy is my act of faith that the prayers could be answered one day.

Many years ago, before my stroke, I was part of an emerging leaders group at church run by Pastor Stuart. We were talking about the Pentecostal Fourfold Gospel. 'Jesus is our Saviour, he is our baptiser, he is our healer and he is the coming King.' Stuart said people seem to struggle more believing that God is our healer than believing the others. He asked us why we thought that was. I remember Stuart's face when I flippantly answered back, 'Because he doesn't heal anymore.' I didn't mean this to sound so faithless and controversial. I was thinking if a person is told 'God is healer' but in their experience he has allowed a family member to suffer and die with little or no relief, I could understand their reluctance to accept that description.

I think we can sometimes invite cynicism in the way we attribute the recovery of disease to God. Imagine with me the scene. A lady in church gets up to speak. She wants to give testimony to the divine healing God has provided. She briefly describes how she took the drugs she was asked to and that after a year God had healed her as a response to her many hours of prayer and fasting. Now imagine that my non-Christian friend is attending with me. His mother had the same cancer and the same excellent treatment and had recovered in a similar time. She hadn't prayed though and yet still got better. Sitting in church now, wouldn't he feel a little bit cynical about the role God had in the two ladies' physical healings? When we do give testimony, unless there has been an undeniable miracle that cannot be explained by medical science, perhaps we should pay more attention to the comfort and courage we had knowing that God was with us in our suffering, supporting us by his word and through the church. We should not feel we need to downplay the professionalism of the medical team and the innovative new drugs that led to our healing. Of course we can give thanks to God ultimately for our healing wrought by the medical profession. Every good gift comes from him and it is surely he who created man with the intellect necessary for such medicine.

Suppose one of your neighbours is given the name 'Dave the Fixer of Cars'. You would assume he was given this because he was especially good at mending cars. You wouldn't expect him to be just a run-of-the-mill mechanic. If his whole identity was as someone who fixes cars, you would expect him to be a cut above the average. You could then become a little bit jaded if you found out that actually there was a pretty big proportion of cars that he didn't fix. And compared to going to a mechanic he was a pretty bad choice if your car was broken.

I would have to agree that this would be a reasonable comparison to God as the fixer of bodies! If your body is broken and you want it mended, going to see a doctor would be more effective than attending a prayer meeting. The difference is God is our healer and is not just the fixer of our bodies; the healing he offers is far more profound than merely our physical state. As well as physical healings that people do attest to, he is also our provider and sustainer. Fixing someone physically demonstrates God's ability to heal physically but it does nothing to demonstrate these other attributes. How can God show his provision without need and how does he show that he is our sustainer without permitting a long-term struggle?

In the early 1900s or in rural Africa, people did and do attest to God's provision more frequently coming in the form of a miraculous healing. This shouldn't be dismissed as a phenomenon owing to their lack of enlightened Western education. Firstly, seeing a doctor in the early 1900s did not give you any immediate expectation of being cured. Furthermore, in rural Africa, having to walk for three days to see a doctor or requiring an amount of money that could never be raised might render 21st-century healthcare beyond reach, making a direct miracle often the only means by which God could enact healing.

My dad used to say he wasn't afraid of heights or even falling but he was afraid of the sudden stop when he hit the ground! Some people desire money but it's reasonable to conclude it's not actually the pieces of paper that they want, but rather the happiness they believe they will get if they have more money. I would argue the same about physical healing. What I really desire is to be able to do the things I used to be able to do that made me really happy and content. What if God could give you the joy and contentment without the physical 'fixing' you thought was necessary?

I want to correct the record that I am not claiming that I live in a state of constant contentment. I do, however, believe that the increasing glimpses of contentment I feel today could one day coalesce into a life where I am truly content in all circumstances. Despite Paul's repeated persecution and incarcerations, he said he was able to say:

'I am not saying this because I am in need, for I have learned to be content whatever the circumstances. I know what it is to be in need, and I know what it is to have plenty. I have learned the secret of being content in any and every situation, whether well fed or hungry, whether living in plenty or in want. I can do all this through him who gives me strength.' (Philippians 4:11-13)

This quote from Paul takes us nicely back to the first century. A few years before Paul wrote these words Jesus was travelling around healing people wherever he went. Can any of Jesus' miraculous healings tell the 21st-century church how it should treat people with disabilities?

6
WHY Did Jesus Heal?

When Jesus walked the earth his teaching was accompanied by many signs and wonders, not least a prolific healing ministry. In fact, healing the sick was a massive part of Jesus' ministry and not just people getting better over time with his help but sudden miraculous changes.

When Jesus said, 'You will do even greater things' (John 14:12) was he talking about these miraculous healings? Jesus was both an example for Christians to follow but he was also God, so were all his healings examples for Christians to follow or were some of them signs to simply show he was God?

As a global church our effectiveness at healing disease, ending suffering and turning people towards God is massively more substantial than what Jesus achieved as one man in Palestine 2,000 years ago. This is what Jesus meant when he said, 'You will do even greater things.' He wasn't expecting every individual Christian to do greater works than God himself but the church as Christ's body was expected to do greater as a whole.

When a person was disabled in the first century it meant something quite different to what it does today. There was certainly no technology or equipment to mitigate their challenges but in addition there was a widespread belief that they deserved it and consequently they were shunned and excluded by the community. In order for God to restore this person to their community, in fact to make it possible that this person could even enter a place of worship, he would have to first deal with the physical ailment. It was the restoration of the person that God wanted to achieve, the physical healing was just one of the ways in which he did it. Some disabled people in the UK may feel that they are still excluded by society on some occasions today but it is not the same degree of conscious exclusion as it was for people living in the first century.

I want to look at some of the healings Jesus performed and pick out certain aspects of these accounts which may point towards something God is telling us about healing today.

In the gospel of John Jesus meets a blind man. We don't know much about him except that he was blind from birth. I have already said that if somebody had a disability in the first century then it was understood that they must have done something to deserve it. Therefore the disciples asked a very logical question: 'If he was born like this then was it his sin or his parents?' (see John 9:2). They rightly concluded that it couldn't really be his fault if he was only a baby but it also seemed grossly unfair and against everything they had hitherto learned from Jesus about his Father that he would afflict somebody because of someone else's sin. This wasn't the just Father they had been hearing about.

In a moment, Jesus overturned centuries of understanding about disability and confirmed that the disciples' confusion was indeed justified.

> 'Neither this man nor his parents sinned . . . but this happened so
> that the works of God might be displayed in him.' (John 9:3)

Jesus then proceeded to heal the man and display God's power as he promised. He did this only as a sign to show he had the authority to overturn centuries-old ideas that disability must have some origin in personal sin.

In Mark's gospel chapter 10 we hear about another blind man. We don't know much about this man either, but there is no evidence to suggest it's the same person. His name was Bartimaeus. Bartimaeus was sitting at the side of the road begging when Jesus and his entourage passed by. Realising his opportunity to be healed, Bartimaeus began shouting, 'Jesus, son of David, have mercy on me' (v. 47). Many people told him to be quiet. Of course they would have thought that his blindness was evidence that he wasn't a good man so they would want to keep him away from the great work Jesus was doing. Jesus heard him and asked that he was brought to him. He then said something which is a lesson for all of us today but at the time it must have been bizarre. He said, 'What do you want me to do for you?' Surely it was obvious! At the time people must have wondered what on earth he was talking about but even now, in the 21st century, if somebody has a disability and requests prayer people assume it's obvious what they really want. If the disabled person were to ask for anything other than total immediate healing, might the pray-er believe this is just due to lack of faith? Would asking for prayer for care provision just be the faithless action of somebody who really wants much more?

In this story Bartimaeus did want to see and had faith that this was possible. There is no indication that the amount of faith made the healing possible but certainly the presence of faith was mentioned by Jesus. I have a friend who had the exact experience I described a moment ago. She was having a meeting about the care package that was being negotiated for her and she went forward to receive prayer that she would have favour in the meeting. The pastor tried to encourage her. 'I'm not going to pray for that; I believe God can do a full healing. That will be my prayer.' My friend didn't get up and walk but she also didn't receive prayer for what she needed.

Mark and Luke both tell us about a paralysed man who was healed. He was carried on a mat by his friends to meet Jesus but they couldn't get near him, so they made a hole in the roof of the building where Jesus was teaching and lowered him down right in front of Jesus. Once again Jesus comments on the presence of faith. It is not clear exactly what the nature of the relationship between healing and faith is, but in this case the faith of the disabled man wasn't mentioned at all and it was his friends' faith that moved God. I remember when I was first unwell this story comforted me. It signalled to me that even if I had almost no faith whatsoever, the faith of my friends and family would mean that my lack of faith could never be the reason for God not acting.

Jesus was never lacking in compassion but it seems that he rarely if ever healed someone purely out of compassion. This sounds surprising but there was always an additional reason. When Jesus saw the man lying in front of him with enormous physical needs he chose to say, 'Your sins are forgiven.' The people around must have thought, well obviously they are not forgiven because he's still lying there! Remember, if anyone was disabled it was because of their sin, so if Jesus really had forgiven his sins the people thought it would be evident from the fact that he got better. Jesus deliberately left the man unhealed for a little bit longer just to make the point that it was possible that somebody could still be disabled even after Jesus declared him righteous in his presence. The subsequent healing was merely a sign to prove to the Pharisees and the crowd that he really did have the authority to forgive sins.

There was a pool called Bethesda where crowds of disabled and sick people would gather. There was a belief that if the waters were stirred by an angel then the first person who made it into the waters would be healed. There's a story in John chapter 5, telling of when Jesus went to this pool. What is striking is that Jesus seems to have ignored the multitudes of people and left them to their beliefs which may have been no more than superstition; where was the compassion for all those people? He approached just one man and asked, 'Do you want to be well?' The man explained a few reasons why this wasn't possible but confirmed that indeed he was trying to get healing, so Jesus healed him there and then. This gives another intriguing dimension to the question of faith. The man who was healed didn't even know who Jesus was, let alone have faith in him! Later on Jesus sees the man again and says something that has been misinterpreted many times. Jesus says, 'Stop sinning or something worse will happen.' This would have fitted quite nicely with the beliefs of certain people. They thought the man must have done something bad otherwise he wouldn't have been disabled in the first place. They believed by great fortune Jesus had forgiven and healed him, and was now warning him that if he sinned again God would inflict on him an even greater disability. I don't believe this was what Jesus meant. I don't think he was warning the man that committing another sin would undo the healing but that going back to a life of sin would have a much graver consequence. The consequence he was talking about was not merely disability in this life but eternal separation from God.

This does not mean that the consequences of sin are only felt in eternity. C.S. Lewis suggested that 80 per cent of suffering in this world can be attributed to sin. However, these are direct consequences caused by sinful actions. For example, somebody could be suffering with a sore leg but if the sore leg was caused by me kicking them, obviously there is a direct link between my sin and his suffering. It is not the case that God causes suffering as a deterrent to sin and, on the very rare occasion that God uses some degree of discomfort as a means to get our attention, there is no evidence that he has ever caused permanent disability for this purpose.

In Genesis there is a story in which God appears to permanently injure Jacob's hip. I thought this required some explanation. When you or I read a story in the Old Testament, we most likely come to it with the foreknowledge of the revelation of Jesus, the teachings of Paul and the experience of countless Christians and theologians throughout the centuries. We also have the context of the whole of the Old Testament to help us understand the character of God. Consequently, when we read an individual story in isolation, it can seem to really jar with what we thought we knew. For example, why did God order the slaughter of tens of thousands of people and how can we reconcile the loving God with the account of Abraham being told to sacrifice his son? When I'm reading the Old Testament I find it useful to consider what people of that time would have expected to be recorded. For example, people believed that there were a number of gods and that the power of an individual god could be measured by the success of their nation. It would therefore not be surprising for the original audience to hear a patriotic account amplify the military successes and attribute them to their god. However, amongst all the genealogies and talk of battles, the Old Testament also includes totally unexpected scenarios that should grab our attention.

The story in which Jacob wrestles with a man all night but then realises in the morning that he had actually been wrestling with God himself, is just one of those unexpected situations. This story would have told the original audience that Yahweh, the god of the Hebrews, was not like other gods. Up until this point, Abraham's god was just one amongst many. However, by this time, when Jacob is on the verge of entering the promised land and fulfilling the Abrahamic covenant, this story signified a tipping point when Jacob realises that Yahweh is quite different. Before this time it would have been inconceivable to anyone that a mortal man could so much as influence one of the gods, let alone wrestle with one and survive. In this account God reaches out and gently touches Jacob's hip, but even this delicate gesture was enough to cause a permanent limp. Jacob considered the injury to be a gift to remind him that he had been in the presence of God all night and lived. This action by God could be an indication that he was now choosing to redeem disability. It would be easy to think that when considering the purity needed for sacrifices or the perfections demanded by the law, God required flawlessness. In this story, just before he renames Jacob, Israel, as patriarch of Yahweh's chosen people, he does something unthinkable for the people at that time. He gives Jacob a physical limitation as a badge of honour.

When Jesus rose again, he still bore the scars from his crucifixion. It might have been expected that when Jesus reappeared with his new 'perfect' body it would be flawless. Perhaps Yahweh's idea of perfection is different from ours.

So back to the healings of Jesus. These healings were primarily signs that indicated Jesus's divinity. As 21st-century Christians we are not expected to simply imitate the words and actions of Jesus to get the same results. Instead we may pray. But should we fast when we pray? Should we recite Scripture? Pray to saints? Or just pray persistently?

7
A Lesson from Paul

Oskar Schindler was an unremarkable man before the Second World War. He was a womaniser and a profiteer and not the obvious person to be given the title Righteous Among the Nations by the Yad Vashem Holocaust Museum in Jerusalem. His business was making enamelware and ammunition for the Nazi war machine in Krakow, Poland. He employed Jews from the local ghetto. When the Jews were due to be sent to the death camps, he bribed officials to keep his employees and he moved them to a camp in the relatively safer Czechoslovakia. At the end of the war he was penniless but had saved over 1,100 Jews.

In the famous Steven Spielberg film of Schindler's life, there were numerous powerful scenes and yet amongst the horror and disbelief that this was actually based on a true story, there was one scene that really made me think, and it's probably not one of the ones you would expect. In the film, at the end of the war, just before the Allied soldiers arrive at the town where Oskar Schindler's factory was in Czechoslovakia, he himself was trying to escape. Despite all his great works he was still actually a member of the Nazi Party and as such would have been arrested or killed by any liberating army. His workers knew that he had saved their lives so they all came out to say farewell. They wrote a note to explain how good he had been to them and they wanted to show their appreciation for what he had done. Schindler had done something so selfless; he had saved over 1,100 Jews, literally spending his own wealth buying their lives from the Nazis. He has been known through generations for his incredible actions but in this scene, as he gets into his car, he says, 'Why did I keep this car. I could have saved ten more lives,' and then he takes off a brooch, looks at it and says, 'That's one more. I could have saved one more.'

However generous or selfless or righteous somebody is they could always do more. This is a challenge for Christians. We may feel that simply going to church on a Sunday isn't really enough to call ourselves Christians but if we go to church on Sunday, go to a prayer meeting in the week and then attend a local home group, is this enough? Maybe we should pray for half an hour every day? But is that enough? Maybe we should be volunteering on one of our free nights and perhaps half an hour prayer simply isn't enough. This can go on and on. What is enough?

There are many doctrines adopted by the church that are said to further the effectiveness of prayers. Some are advocated by Jesus, such as fasting, but others have seemingly been adopted with little biblical basis. It feeds into this cycle of how much is really enough. I want to challenge the perceived necessity for prayer to be persistent in order to move God.

If God only responds or is more likely to respond to persistent prayer, how much is necessary? I believe God can bring about a change to our circumstances but what if we're only praying for half an hour a day when the persistence he requires is forty-five minutes a day? If we remain unhealed should we try an hour a day, and if the healing still doesn't come should we keep praying more and more?

I was troubled by this. It would seem a fairly universal belief that we should be persistent in prayer, and so, as I was still unhealed, was it because I wasn't being persistent enough. Then I thought about Paul and his thorn in the flesh. He wasn't persistent. Why not? What was different about him? I decided to do my university dissertation finding out why.

I had grown up hearing messages such as 'if a prayer wasn't answered we should remain persistent about it and not give up'. I listened to a sermon that used those exact words. The preacher actually said, 'If your prayers are not answered you should be either praying more persistently or you're giving up.' So was Paul giving up? He only prayed about his 'thorn in the flesh' three times and then to our knowledge he stopped. Paul tells us he received an answer from God specifically saying, 'My grace is sufficient for you' (2 Corinthians 12:9). We don't know what the 'thorn in the flesh' he was referring to actually was. Some have suggested it was an element of persistent eye problems following his profound blindness during his conversion experience and others have postulated that he could be referring to some human opposition to his ministry. Even if Paul's eye troubles were not the 'thorn in the flesh', most people would accept Paul did in fact have some trouble with his eyes that he doesn't appear to have been praying about.

In my head I imagined Paul attending a 21st-century charismatic service for healing. 'I have been having problems with my eyes for some months now and they seem to be getting worse. I've been praying to God for him to heal me and remove this burden. I haven't just prayed once – I've asked three times – but I get the sense that God doesn't want to make me better; rather he wants to work with my limitations to show his power.' The senior member of the prayer team rests his hand on Paul's shoulder and says, 'God doesn't want you to suffer. You must be persistent and not be discouraged. If you really want God to heal you, you must keep praying until you get a breakthrough.'

If this really is the response Paul would receive in the modern church, where did we go wrong? One explanation is a popular misinterpretation of the parables in Luke 5. Firstly, Jesus tells us to ask for our daily bread but in the following parable a neighbour is reluctant to give his friend any bread; however, when his friend was persistent he eventually gave in and gave him some bread. There is a popular interpretation that suggests that God is similar to the neighbour in that he is more willing to give us our daily bread if we cajole him first. Secondly, there is a story about a poor widow trying to get justice from an unjust judge. One interpretation suggests if the unjust judge eventually relented after the poor widow was persistent, how much more is God going to relent and answer prayer if we don't give up asking? Most of Jesus' parables were essentially showing what God is like, or what the Kingdom of God is like, but these two were unique amongst Jesus' parables because they were actually saying God is not like this.

A misunderstanding of this may have reinforced people's faith in the doctrine of persistence. Perseverance in prayer certainly has its place but it can be misunderstood. An individual could easily believe that if they are merely persistent in petitioning God for their desires, they will in fact be answered positively so long as they do not give up. I once heard that offering prayers that were not persistent was a bit like treating God as a vending machine, where you ask for what you want at that moment and expect God to deliver it. The speaker expanded his point by explaining that if we were persistent God really knew we were serious about what we wanted and would therefore only answer it if we were persistent. I flippantly thought this just sounded like a very stubborn vending machine!

'Do not be anxious about anything, but in everything by prayer and supplication with thanksgiving let your requests be made known to God. And the peace of God, which surpasses all understanding, will guard your hearts and your minds in Christ Jesus.' (Philippians 4:6-7 ESV)

Prayer can often be confused with this persistent asking for things. In the above verses Paul doesn't just say 'by prayer'; he says 'by prayer AND supplication', indicating that he considers the two things to be different. If I said I am buying bedroom furniture AND a bed you could deduce

A Lesson from Paul

the bedroom furniture to which I am referring is not just a bed; it's obviously something in addition to it. So when Paul says prayer, the Greek word he wrote down was *proseuchē* and supplication is translated from *deēsei* so he's obviously considering them both to be different from each other. We know what supplication is – it's asking God for what we want – but what is prayer?

Whenever Paul wanted to indicate that he was praying, he would use the Greek word *proseuchesthe* or a derivative like *proseuchē*, as in the aforementioned Philippians verse, and yet when Paul implored that God remove his thorn he decided not to use either of these words. He was neither praying (*proseuchē*) or supplicating (*deēsei*). Instead he described what he was doing as *parakalesa*. Other derivatives of this word can sometimes indicate a sort of begging but this exact word only appears five times in the New Testament. Only when talking about his thorn did translators translate this as 'implore'; elsewhere it is said to mean 'requested', 'encouraged' or 'urged'. I think Paul ASKED. Presumably, in order to get the answer, he did pray, but this was prayer seeking God and not just petitioning him for the answer he desired.

The biblical text also says in Luke 11:9-10:

> 'So I say to you: ask and it will be given to you; seek and you will find; knock and the door will be opened to you. For everyone who asks receives; the one who seeks finds; and to the one who knocks, the door will be opened.'

Reading this scripture on one level you could think it's giving you three different words that all mean prayer or supplication, but I believe asking, seeking and knocking were not the same but referred to different aspects of communication with God. If asking is not actually prayer at all but something else, then seeking is prayer where the pray-er seeks God rather than seeking the things God can do or only seeking his answer to whether God is going to do what they want. Finally, knocking is a way of prayerfully aligning one's own will with the will of God.

Asking

Firstly, Christians are encouraged to ask. God wants to know the desires of his people. In Isaiah 7:11 (MSG), God tells Ahaz to 'be extravagant ... ask for the moon!' In the Garden of Gethsemane Jesus asked that the cup may be taken away, and finally Paul asks that he can be relieved of his affliction.

My grandad used to say that when God answers petitions he sometimes says 'yes', he sometimes says 'no', and he sometimes says 'not yet'. If God responds 'yes' to an initial 'ask' request, this should be fairly evident as the prayer has just been answered in the way it was requested. However, if it is not answered straight away, the pray-er does not know if God has said 'no' or 'not yet'. In their subsequent prayers, when they are earnestly 'seeking' God's presence, an answer may be forthcoming.

Seeking

Prayer is supposed to be dialogical and not just a repetitive monologue to God. You cannot force God's arm by pestering for something that is against God's will; contrary to the misinterpretations of the parables in Luke, we must first seek his will. This is where some persistence may in fact be required. By persistently seeking God's presence, his will becomes apparent; it can make decades of prayers more effective by not petitioning for something repeatedly which is opposed to God's purpose. It was during his 'seeking' that Paul heard God saying, 'My grace is sufficient for you' (2 Corinthians 12:9).

Seeking involves earnestly looking for God's will, not just considering it. Seeking God's will is making the initial request subservient to what he thinks is best. Although some people warn that adding the obligatory 'if it's your will' to the end of a prayer is admitting a lack of faith that your persistence may not prevail, it is inconceivable that any true Christian would advocate 'not making' a prayer subject to God's will so this is unlikely to be what they mean. More likely, they are warning against using 'according to your will' as an easy way of explaining the reason for unanswered prayer, without having to consider the real reasons. In rare circumstances there may be some behavioural change required but if you are taught to totally dismiss any other reason for unanswered prayer by saying, 'Well, it must not be God's will,' then we are removing a very valuable way in which God sometimes gets our attention. However, this is clumsy and preachers could be misinterpreted and understood to be saying that seeking God's will is somehow watering down the initial request. Actually, I believe making any petition subservient to God's will should never be discouraged for any reason. Now what should be described as persistence occurs only when Christians enter the 'knocking' part of prayer.

Knocking

When a person first seeks God's presence and then discovers his will, he may receive an answer similar to Paul, 'My grace is sufficient for you'; this is God saying, 'No.' God may alternatively acknowledge the suffering and make a promise; it is prayer for this promise to be fulfilled that God may wish his followers to be persistent about. When praying persistently about one of God's promises, that person is reminding themselves of the promise each time they pray. The Greek word translated as 'confess' could also be interpreted as 'to agree with'. For example, when somebody is admitting their sin, they are in effect saying to God, 'Despite what I have done, I now wish to assert that I was wrong, and I still choose to believe that what you say is sin I also consider to be sin.' Similarly, persistently praying for something that has already been promised by God is a way of repeatedly aligning one's own will with that promise.

The disciples in the upper room had a promise from Jesus and decided, as a result of this promise, they would persistently pray for it until it was realised. In Daniel 10:12-13 Gabriel said God heard and answered Daniel's prayer straight away; there was no suggestion that he only heard it after persistence. It was Gabriel himself who was delayed delivering the answer as he was detained by the Prince of Persia. Here there is not a suggestion that God's ability to answer the petition was being hindered by the demonic forces, so, obviously, if God had already answered his petition positively, asking again and again is not going to help Gabriel to deliver it more quickly. If a person orders a parcel and that parcel is dispatched and then subsequently held up in transit, continually calling the original seller is not going to clear the blockage as the parcel has already been dispatched.

Prayer surrounding long-term disability hinges on seeking God. It's important when we are seeking God that we check ourselves and make sure we are not just seeking the things we want from God. It's when we seek God that he is able to reassure us of his love and acceptance of how we are or make us aware of something in our lives that needs to change. If we are repeatedly petitioning and only waiting to hear the word 'Yes' then we're going to fail to hear the other things God may wish to say. This may indeed be a promise for our healing but if it is, we can then pray persistently with faith rather than petitioning in an ever more desperate way for God to hear us.

I had another thought: most Christians would agree that God is both omnipotent (all-powerful) and omni-benevolent (all-good). God would therefore know what his people need and wish to do it; any supplications would therefore be futile as God would already be doing the very best anyway. C.S. Lewis suggests that as well as God's omni-characteristics, humans have free will and can therefore influence the execution of God's purposes. Persistent prayer without a promise from God throws up a potential harm.

We know that petitionary prayer can be effective, which means God must be doing some things that are dependent on our prayer and not simply doing what he knows is best. More likely he is encouraging us to pray for the right things so he can then deliver it, but if prayer is to have any purpose he would have to be willing to withhold the blessings – but for the right prayer.

This is an uncomfortable idea. If we believe God knows what's best and will do it whatever we do, what would be the point in asking for anything? If God is indeed willing to withhold his best because we do not ask, is it possible that repeatedly asking for something, irrespective of what God's will might be, could he eventually just give us what we're asking for rather than giving us his best? A friend, when proof-reading this chapter, wrote: 'May not the actual process of prayer [regardless of specific purpose in the mind of the one supplicating] have an entirely different rationale from God's perspective? Perhaps the need to remind us that we are mortal and dependent creatures, ontologically different from God. Maybe the idea is that of developing a relationship – the old idea of seeking the Giver rather than the gift.'

8
A Lesson from the Medical Profession

So far I have talked about some of the things the church doesn't get right and I may have neglected to emphasise how incredible both the God we serve and the church community are. I thought about what principles the church could adopt to avoid the rare but painful experiences I have described so far.

My mind is drawn back to my professional ethics that were an important guiding principle to my work as a dentist for many years. Contrary to popular belief, doctors are no longer required to take the Hippocratic Oath, but the four pillars of medical ethics that were derived from this are still an important guiding framework for doctors, dentists and other medical professionals. It was my high regard for these ethical pillars that made me reflect about how I was treated by church leaders and individuals who responded in a compassionate and constructive manner. I then considered whether these four medical moral principles could be consciously applied to Christian ministry.

Hippocrates' first principle is *autonomy*. This is a commitment to grant the patient their own choice regardless of whether it goes against what the expert deems is best for the patient. As a dentist I would frequently suggest something which wasn't popular with my patient but I saw it as my responsibility to try to educate them so that they would ultimately see my logic and consent to treatment. However, if they still insisted that they didn't agree I would always respect their autonomy.

I remember realising the gravity of autonomy when I was given it for another human being. For a time I used to do general anaesthetic work in hospital, which primarily involved taking out children's teeth when they had become too damaged to save. A couple of these general anaesthetic sessions were designated for treating people with special needs. Because these people were often not very compliant to examinations, a decision had to be made while they were asleep as to what treatment would be most appropriate. On the face of it this sounds like the perfect situation for a busy dentist where you can just get on and do what you believe is the right thing without having to explain yourself. It took me by surprise just how uncomfortable I felt taking away autonomy for another human being. I was desperate for someone to question my decision and ultimately take the responsibility away from me.

Autonomy is a well-understood principle in Christianity; we call it free will. God has given us free will (possibly the most extreme autonomy) so we are allowed to do whatever we choose despite the consequences.

The next principle is *beneficence*. This is a principle that may have to be balanced with autonomy. Fairly regularly during my career someone would ask me to take out all of their teeth and make dentures. They were quite clear about what they wanted and if I was to simply give them unfettered autonomy I could just do as they asked and, incidentally, make more money by simply agreeing. This is where the principle of beneficence is really important for a professional. Because of my years of training and experience I knew too well the consequences of just removing the natural teeth and replacing them with plastic ones. I often used to quote somebody I had heard who said dentures can be an excellent provision for someone with no teeth but they are a fairly poor replacement for your own teeth. When faced with someone wanting me to take out all their teeth and replace them, I would try to convince them that dentures weren't the best option and I would try to change their mind. But, ultimately, if I couldn't I would consider the principle of beneficence (doing the best for my patient) as more important than simply doing as they asked. If we couldn't come to an agreement, ultimately I would do nothing.

Once again this is a principle the church understands well. We believe in a benevolent God who desires the very best for all people. When we pray to God we express our desires but we also trust that God has our best interests at heart. He may do what we ask, however if he doesn't think it's going to be to our benefit he won't necessarily do what we ask, and we trust this is God acting in our best interests and not just refusing to help. Likewise in the church, we should endeavour to meet people's requests for help but when what they ask is clearly contrary to their interest or our conscience then we are not obliged to do it.

The third pillar of medical ethics is *justice*. I suppose this could be seen as equity rather than equality. For example, the NHS spends more money looking after me than they spend looking after most people, but rather than treating everyone exactly the same, justice dictates we should treat people fairly, so if someone's needs are greater, there is more help available. Justice is also treating people of different races or gender equitably. God made it clear he considers all people to be equal, and loves and treats us all fairly whether we believe in Jesus or not, but that doesn't mean he treats everyone exactly the same.

Finally, the last pillar is *non-maleficence*. For an example of this principle I wanted to explain a dilemma a little bit closer to home. My stroke took effect in two stages about eighteen hours apart. After the first stage I could have been given clot-busting drugs to dissolve the blood clot forming in my brain, and in hindsight I now know this may have mitigated the effect of my stroke. However, my doctors, while knowing the benefits of doing this, would have also had to consider the potential harm this action may have caused. The blood clot had been formed by an injury to my neck and the only thing stopping me

bleeding to death from that injury was another blood clot. My doctors would have faced the dilemma of balancing beneficence with non-maleficence. Giving the drugs would certainly have a benefit against my stroke but if this meant I also bled to death they would have to take into account this potential harm.

Now I want to consider praying for the sick and explore how these principles may influence our behaviour.

Firstly autonomy: as dentists when we were examining patients we wouldn't ask every patient to sign a consent form before we even looked at them. Instead we would use what we called implied consent; by this I mean if someone attended the dentist, sat in the chair and laid back with their mouth open, we could assume they were consenting to non-invasive treatment. Likewise, if a person attends a healing crusade and goes forward for prayer it would be a reasonable assumption that they don't mind being prayed for. If someone was to simply ask, 'Can I pray for you?' this wouldn't seem unreasonable.

In an earlier chapter I shared a story about one of my experiences at church. Simply attending a church is not giving consent to anybody who wishes to lay hands on me to do so and begin praying. A blind BBC reporter in an article 'Stop Trying to Heal Me' accounts how he and other disabled people can feel uncomfortable when they are out in public and a Christian randomly offers to pray for physical healing, saying it had 'put him off Christianity'.

This also happened to me just the other day. I was enjoying an afternoon in the nice weather with my carer; we stopped for a drink and were then walking home through the park. Ironically, when I am walking through the park on a nice day I often feel overwhelmed by just how blessed I am to live in such a beautiful area and for the people in my life. An elderly gentleman, who obviously didn't think I looked particularly blessed, interrupted our walk and said, 'Excuse me, do you know Jesus?'

Both my carer and I stopped what we were doing and both said, 'Yes.'

He then said, 'But do you believe he can heal you?'

I looked at him and said, 'Yes, I do.'

He looked a bit taken off guard but continued with his routine. 'Jesus said just have faith and you will be healed.'

Clearly a little irritated my carer said, 'Actually, Andy knows what Jesus said; he has a degree in Theology and is writing a book about healing!'

He came back quickly and said, 'I'm not talking about Theology, do you know Jesus in your heart?'

I was a little offended and hurt so I asked him, 'Do you think I need healing more than you do?'

He was silent for quite a while and then he quickly reached out his hand, touched my shoulder and said, 'In Jesus' name get up and walk,' and then quickly scurried off muttering to himself.

These experiences still leave me feeling a bit rubbish. I don't want people to look at me in the park and assume I don't know Jesus because I'm in a wheelchair. Thankfully, just five minutes later a member of our own church came cycling towards me. I did not recognise her because of her sunglasses but she saw me, stopped her bike, took off her glasses and was beaming at the chance encounter and the opportunity to catch up. It was so normal just to be able to talk about my young family and when we would get back to church. I could have been anyone.

How should justice affect the church? Along with our salvation, God gave us spiritual gifts including the gift of administering his healing power. Do we sometimes only use our gifts to bless one another in church rather than taking our gifts, including healing, to the people most in need? Justice would imply that our spiritual gifts should be used to benefit those in most need wherever they happen to be; however, as I explained previously, autonomy and appropriateness should quite rightly prevent us from doing this without much prayer and careful thought.

The man in the park was showing that he really understood the principles of justice and benevolence. He understood that God hasn't given spiritual gifts just so that Christians can bless each other in church but he intends Christians to take those gifts, including the gift of healing, out into the community to bless the people most in need. Where I believe his actions were unwise is that he failed to balance all four ethical pillars properly. If you imagine a table with four legs and each leg is a different ethical pillar, all four need to be perfectly balanced or the table won't be level. In the case of this man, the pillars of autonomy and non-malevolence were not in place at all, causing the table to fall over.

This demonstrates the tension between how the four principles are balanced. Perhaps an appropriate compromise could be that Christians wanting to offer to pray for individuals in their community could set up a stand offering prayer but not actively approach 'needy' looking people. This would give people the autonomy to request prayer if they wish and allow them to specify their own perceived needs. It would avoid disabled people feeling anxious when approaching such a stand for fear that they could be made a spectacle of. I believe the ministry 'Healing on the Streets' (the ministry founded by Mark Marx in Coleraine) aims to do this. They pray before they start and ask God to send the right people to them. When they pray for people they ask them what they want prayer for, and their key principles are gentleness, respect and compassion. Unfortunately, there are copycat ministries that say they are *doing* healing on the streets who operate quite differently. They will scan the high street for people in wheelchairs, mobility scooters and people with guide dogs, effectively trying to identify who they think are most needy. They then offer to pray similarly to the man in my local park. Emma tells me Slimming World is effective for many people but we don't expect her or representatives of Slimming World to be approaching unsuspecting overweight people in the high street and offering to help!

We often hear about God being a benevolent God but actually he's a perfect example of someone who balances beneficence with non-maleficence. When we consider praying for healing, the beneficent thing to do is obvious; if we know that our prayer could potentially help someone to get well, then surely we should pray. There are all sorts of examples in the Bible where additional things are done that seemed to make prayer for healing more effective, for example should we be anointing people with oil? Is there an advantage when certain people pray? What about fasting, prayer handkerchiefs and increasing faith? These are all things which people believe may increase the likelihood of healing so if we're being completely beneficent should we not try them all, just in case one of them persuades God to unlock his healing power?

A purely beneficent approach would require us to do everything we can do to increase the likelihood of healing and pay no regard to the potential harm it causes if the healing doesn't occur either at all or in a way we expect.

The final principle, non-maleficence (do no harm), is where I believe some churches dangerously part ways from the medical profession. In my experience, non-maleficence is rarely considered by churches who regularly pray for the supernatural but even when it is, it can be discouraged as an admission of doubt. It would seem that whenever such churches take action they only consider the potential benefits of their approach to healing and do not sufficiently weigh the potential harm that may be caused. An example of this is when someone seems blinkered, imagining the glory of witnessing a healing and ending my suffering. If, in their opinion, the likelihood of this is increased by inflating faith or heightening expectation, then they think this should be done. At no point do they consider the hurt they may inflict. In my case the harm ranged from just feeling self-conscious and the centre of attention to seriously risking the loss of my faith. For nearly a year I remained convinced that God would heal me. Despite the more and more unlikely this seemed, I would be congratulated by people for my faith whenever I indicated I still thought it would happen. When it didn't, I was left with an overwhelming sense of guilt that I had let others down by not giving them the miraculous healing they had been praying so faithfully for. During my darkest moments, I feared that, despite my previously strong conviction, there must not be a God after all. I was lucky that, with my friends' and family's encouragement, I enrolled on a Theology degree which helped to restore my faith but how many formerly committed Christians are hopelessly damaged by the same type of experiences?

If a person presents for healing we must pray but we have no way of knowing that our prayer will result in healing and, even if it does, we don't know how this healing will look. We should never focus purely on the benefits of a particular action and spare scant or no regard for the feelings of the person we are praying for.

9

A Better Way

There isn't a specific time when faithful hope becomes destructive denial. There are many examples of hope continuing despite a terminal diagnosis and that hope being justified when, against all medical predictions, the person recovers. However, it's also the case that the most faithful Christians can receive a terminal diagnosis and the disease progresses pretty much as the experts would expect despite hours of intercession. 'Precious in the sight of the LORD is the death of his saints' (Psalm 116:15 KJV). A Christian and their family should have no fear in the dying stage but if they are taught to believe that they should have faith to overcome the dying process and that a miracle is the only just result, then they may be robbed of the comfort that is rightfully theirs as followers of Christ. What is more, their family may be denied the ability to prepare for death and the after effects of grief could be compounded. I think that there may be many examples of this within churches who regularly heighten faith for healing. It is a topic that is not spoken of from the platform in such churches so congregations may only be hearing of the times where faith for healing is successful.

Emma and I know of quite a few people who have had their grieving process damaged by their belief that they should have faith for healing. One friend of ours received the news that her mother was terminally ill. Not all of her family went to church; some had belief but were not committed Christians. Our friend knew someone who had the faith to pray for the miraculous and had reported healings. He travelled to see her mother and prayed with her and told the whole family to just believe and that the mum would be healed. Our friend felt a great burden to uphold this belief on behalf of her whole family. It had been prophesied and she daren't accept any other interpretation. At every hospital appointment, even when her mother was visibly deteriorating before her, she held onto this belief and refuted doctors when they encouraged her to prepare for her mother's passing. In hope, the whole family believed that her mother would recover. As time progressed and as her mother was dying, our friend experienced intense guilt, fearing a lack of faith on her part which made her feel quite unwell. We encouraged her to go back to the person that prayed with her and clarify whether he had responded to a specific word from God or whether he was simply expressing his own desire that she would be healed. It was the latter, and because our friend was a mature Christian she was able to work through this and accept that God might want to take her mum and was able to grieve appropriately.

Psychologists tell us there are five stages of grief: the first is denial, then anger, bargaining, depression and, finally, acceptance. These are completely normal but it's important that somebody is able to move through all five stages and not get stuck. For example, if someone dies, it would be quite normal to expect disbelief when you first hear the news, but at their funeral you wouldn't expect the pastor to unscrew the coffin and announce, 'They're not dead, they're only sleeping!' This would be returning to denial. I realised rejecting that my disability was permanent wasn't resilient faith but simply a denial. Unless I allowed myself to grieve properly for my old life, I was never going to reach acceptance. Narrowing my pursuit of God to a reality-denying instantaneous healing was preventing God supporting me through the grieving process, allowing me to accept what I now had and using it the best way I could. For a few years now I have been able to accept my disability. Accepting is not stopping mourning the old life and it's not giving up hope, but the hope is now in God and his goodness rather than the things I believe God could do if I convince him that he should.

Matthew and Luke share one of Jesus' parables about a master giving his servants talents for them to steward while he was away. In the Bible a talent was a specific amount of money. The first two stewards used the talents they were given, invested them and were able to give a return. The amounts they were given, and the returns they achieved, were different but the master was happy with both of them because they used what they had wisely. On the other hand, the third man was only given one talent. Realising this wasn't very much, which might have made him perceive the master as 'cruel', he buried it, meaning that what little he still could have done, he didn't do. Perhaps this man thought that if he had been given more talents, like the other stewards, he too would have been able to achieve a return, but perhaps it was his pursuit of more talents which meant he didn't use what he had been given. Imagine if the unwise steward had formed this conclusion because throughout the time the master was away, the other stewards had told him that he should have more or he should be like them and that he couldn't get a return until he had the same as they did with which to work. Perhaps they might tell him to pray for his lot to be changed and to bury the single talent, while he pursued more as a starting point for his investment. This, I feel, is what some churches can do when they alienate disabled people and imply that all Christians should be healthy. In doing this they are inadvertently devaluing the unique gifts that disabled people have to offer.

A friend of ours who has a child with a complex disability explained how, in his experience, individuals often projected their own view of what a successful life should be when praying for his child and he felt in doing so they were trying to change the very thing that made him who he was. They were missing that it was because of his disability that he was so uniquely gifted in unseen ways. He couldn't speak, but in prayer

he was able to vocalise utterances so powerful, he clearly had a unique connection with God. He was also very content, didn't hold grudges and had been shielded from the stress and hurts that the world often brings. Other people might have thought he would have been happier if he could just have been more like them but perhaps he and his family didn't want him to be like everyone else?

I suggest that first we should celebrate the differences in our abilities whether physically, emotionally or academically. It is good to hear stories about how people's hardships have been vital in moulding them into the godly person they are today. Some people are depressed by their particular limitation and we are told to weep with those who weep and rejoice with those who rejoice, so if someone in our church family is weeping we shouldn't pressure them to be hyped up in a service of rejoicing and celebration. It's important to emphasise the fact that Jesus can and does step in to a situation with miraculous power but we also need to champion God's phenomenal ability to sustain and provide in other ways for his children.

The kingdom of God has been made possible by Jesus' atonement; this means that the miraculous is possible but God doesn't promise that this will be the norm until his kingdom comes at the end of the age. What he does promise is that he will never leave us. Some people believe that the works of the Spirit, and therefore God's ongoing interventions, ceased after the first century. Presumably they interpret this promise to be a promise that God will always see us in our trials. Others believe God is always standing by, poised and ready to jump into action to pluck us out of our trials whenever we get the recipe of prayers and sacraments correct. I don't want to champion either extreme; I believe God does divinely intervene all the time but this is not always supernatural. If we only notice God when he does the big supernatural miracles we are missing 90 per cent of what God is doing.

In the introduction I mentioned Pete Greig. He speaks about not asking God 'why' but 'where'. Not trying to find out the reason why God caused or allowed something to happen but asking God to reveal where he is in the circumstances. Sadly it is not always the case but a good place to look for God is often in his church.

I am writing in the middle of the Covid-19 lockdown. Asking God why he allowed the pandemic to happen and expecting a clear decisive answer, feels like hitting your head against a brick wall. However, when you stop and ask God to reveal where he is in the crisis, he is all over it. The government has been setting up armies of volunteers to help provide the necessities for those people who are shielding. They have also encouraged neighbours to look out for one another. It's heartening to see that this is what the church already does and now wider society is recognising the value of a closer community. Church services have moved online and a huge number of people who wouldn't attend church are now viewing church services here. Food banks, many of which are run by churches, are seeing additional needs met and whereas many of the things that people have put their faith in have been proved fallible, many Christians are still holding onto the promises of God. Churches have sprung into action doing what they do best but, moreover, people who may never darken the doorway of a church are acting with incredible compassion and generosity, not to mention the bravery of frontline workers. God is everywhere!

10
Samuel (by Emma, Andy's Wife)

'I prayed for this child, and the LORD has granted me what I asked of him.' (1 Samuel 1:27)

An event from scripture that spoke to me when Andy first became unwell was when the Israelites journeyed through the wilderness. God did not rescue them immediately from captivity, in fact they had many struggles still to navigate, but he sustained them in their Exodus. Deuteronomy 29 tells us that during those forty years, their clothes and shoes did not wear out. It was the miracle of God's provision and sustaining power that could easily be overlooked had the Israelites only been looking for complete and instant freedom.

In sharing our story we want to recognise the ways in which God has provided for us, often through seemingly 'normal' means. God has not removed the trial – the enemy of his all-encompassing paralysis still encumbers Andy – however, we have been able to enjoy God's provision in the presence of it (Psalm 23:5). In reading this book, we hope that you too have been able to chart your own journey of God's provision.

For me, the most amazing and joyous gift has been that we've still had the honour of becoming parents and I want to take some time detailing how our lives have been transformed with the birth of our precious son Samuel.

As already outlined in *Pressed But Not Crushed*, I was a mere twenty-six when Andy had the devastating stroke that left him with locked-in syndrome. Married for only three and a half years, having only dated for fourteen months prior to getting hitched, we were still relatively fresh in our relationship. We both had clear plans that one day we would have children but these were not imminent and we were just enjoying married life whilst being committed to progressing our careers and our various responsibilities at church. I had suffered mental ill health from the age of seventeen. Although this was under control, I had had to change my medication on two occasions when we were first married so that it was better suited if I were to become pregnant. In turn, my mental health had taken a battering and it was a further reason as to why we weren't rushing to start a family.

Then came the fateful day in November 2011 when Andy had the brain stem stroke. Immediately the attention was directed starkly away from any such plans or hopes of becoming parents, to the milestones that instantly became mapped out for us: Andy surviving the critical first few months from intensive care to having his tracheotomy removed, to moving to a rehab unit, and eventually coming home and establishing the right care provision. We were now just fighting for the most minimal needs of survival.

It was around two years post stroke that I found myself at a prayer meeting at Renewal Church, Solihull, the church where I grew up. They had powerful evenings of prayer and I would often attend them for spiritual renewal and to petition for our needs. Pastor David Carr, who was leading the meeting, encouraged the congregation to bring before God our deepest hearts' desire. It hadn't been something that I had been prioritising, or indeed focusing on. All our other needs seemed to swallow up any 'frivolous' hopes or yearnings; it was surely prudent to suppress these for fear of disappointment. Yet, in that moment, I had an overwhelming sense that I must voice to God my deepest longing: I would love to have a child.

We all know about the birds and the bees and yet talking about it when disability comes in to play can be really awkward; let's just say that until that time, two years post brain stem stroke, it had not been physically possible for us to conceive. That week, after attending the Tuesday night prayer meeting, we tried to be intimate again and everything, seemingly miraculously, began working. Let's leave it there! We could now hope that one day we might become parents without IVF or other fertility treatment. Some may say that it is sheer coincidence but through the eyes of faith I saw that this was a divine intervention. It ignited in me hope and belief that God was still involved in miraculous means, albeit in ways that we didn't understand.

It was four years from this time until I would actually become pregnant with our precious Samuel. Often we would wonder whether Andy's disability was still rendering us infertile. I had to keep bringing the desire to be a mother back to the Lord and shut down any thought of going down the IVF route. This isn't wrong in and of itself but we just felt that because of our unique challenges, Andy's complex disability and my own proneness to depression, we wanted to be certain that it was right for us to have a family. Somehow our assurance of this was that if it happened naturally, then it must have been God's will and so we could trust him to enable us to overcome our extra challenges.

When we found out that I was pregnant we were overjoyed. We endeavoured to keep it a secret for the first trimester, which was definitely the toughest, but we told our live-in carers; it was difficult to keep it from them when they lived with us.

They say laughter is medicine and we were certainly amused by some people's remarks when they began noticing that I was pregnant. One neighbour seemed incredulous when he spied my growing bump for the first time. In shock, he seemed unable to filter his thoughts and blurted out: 'You're pregnant. What, Andy? I didn't know he had it in him!' To make things even more awkward, he proceeded to call his friend and recount our predicament! Another instance was when one lady at church was equally surprised to learn that I was expecting and she said to me in front of Andy, 'Does he know?' We had to laugh. I thought to myself, 'Well, yes, he did have something to do with it.' It indicates how some people still assume that Andy's cognition isn't intact because he is so physically disabled, despite them being aware that he was, at the time, completing another degree and had already had a book published.

Hindsight is a wonderful thing. Looking back I can see through the eyes of faith that things were slotting into place for us to be able to provide for our miracle baby Samuel. Ironically, many of these blessings have come about as a direct consequence of Andy's disability. Of course there are many frustrations and pains wrought by Andy's disability and I will detail these later. But firstly, I want to give thanks for the many 'coincidences' which have enabled us to provide Samuel with a loving and stable home in which we trust he will thrive. Many seemed to come about at just the right time after four years of us trying to conceive.

Andy came home in September 2012 but it wasn't until June 2016 that we finished having a purpose-built apartment in our garden. Until then, live-in carers stayed in the bedroom next to us, which was manageable for the time but wouldn't be suited for family life, either for them or us. We needed space and they needed sleep!

We were still pushing Andy in a manual wheelchair, meaning that it would be impossible for us to go out as a family by ourselves without a carer to push. But at Christmas of 2016, we learned about a wheelchair that Andy could control with his head; Andy felt that this was something he could use so we applied for the NHS to provide one. I found out that I was pregnant just a day before the wheelchair assessment appointment, which was so timely, and we were able to discuss what our needs would be as a family of three. We managed to get the chair in good time so that when I became more heavily pregnant I didn't have to continue pushing Andy. We now go out regularly as a family just the three of us (or four if Oni, our dog, comes too!).

It was surely providence that Andy chose to take out the critical health insurance policies when we were first married and a further one just six months before his stroke, thus paying off our mortgage and providing us with a good ongoing income. Although I worked as a teacher, we were never dependent on my salary and so I have been able to take the time off needed whilst Samuel is young to ensure that I am meeting his needs as well as Andy's. We are able to enjoy lots of family time and Samuel has both of us around, which is such a blessing.

In the summer of 2016 we began managing Andy's healthcare budget ourselves, which cut out the expense of employing an agency to do this on our behalf. We could factor into the budget some physiotherapy, which we had previously been paying for and amounted to the monthly outgoing of a mortgage! We decided to put to good use this money and, along with Andy's pension pay-out as a deposit, we bought a holiday home in Dawlish, Devon. The hiring of equipment to go on holiday was almost as expensive as the rental of accommodation and there were very few options of where to go. The purchase of the property was completed in January 2017 and in February 2017 I found out I was pregnant. Looking back I can see how the timing was perfect. With all the needs we had before, it would have been even more difficult to get away with a baby in tow. As well as having the right equipment for Andy, the bungalow meant we could store things like a cot and high chair and get away for family breaks together whenever we wanted. We were able to get the property ready for rental by September 2017 and Samuel was born in the October. It is lovely that we have the bungalow as it is big enough for other family and friends who have children to accompany us and so Samuel gets to spend prolonged time with other children around.

There were concerns around me being pregnant and the post-partum period. There was a history of very severe and complex pre- and post-partum depression within the family, which had had serious effects. I also had already experienced complex mental health issues, for which I was receiving ongoing treatment. In the book *Pressed But Not Crushed*, I detailed how I believe I also experienced a degree of healing around the time when Andy first became poorly, and this had continued. There was still concern I might become ill but I remained well throughout the pre- and post-partum period. I could see God's provision in the close monitoring I had so that early intervention could happen, which meant I didn't have any significant relapse. I also had lots of support from my mum, which was such a blessing

When we were first married we chose the names we hoped to one day call our children: Samuel for a boy, after Andy's great-great-grandfather, and Isabella for a girl, after my grandma. When I was around twelve-weeks pregnant we told my godson that I was having a baby. He straightaway said, 'You'll have a boy and you'll call him Sammy.' Aside, I said to my friend, 'That's what we will call him if he is a boy.' The name Samuel, meaning 'God has heard', is also special to us now because it reminds us of the longing we had for a child, like Hannah in the Old Testament. Samuel's middle name, Joshua, was important as Andy had had prophetic words given to him before and just after the stroke, that he would need to be strong and courageous like Joshua when he took over from Moses. It reminds us of who God has called us to be as a family.

My pregnancy went pretty smoothly until around five months when there was concern over my blood test indicators and I was subsequently diagnosed with obstetric cholestasis: I was secreting bile acids into my blood. One of the symptoms is severe itchiness but it can also be harmful to the baby if gestation goes beyond thirty-seven weeks; I elected for a planned C-section. The day before the operation, Andy's parents had come down to help him navigate the bus route to the hospital in his electric chair. We didn't have a wheelchair-accessible vehicle and so this was the route he would have to take the following day to be there with me at the birth. Meanwhile, I was at the hospital for various pre-op appointments. It was late in the day, my appointments were behind schedule and my parking had already run out. I had been put on a monitor to check baby's heart rate when the midwife voiced her concerns that it was low before calling for a doctor. I was informed that I would have to have a C-section that night. Standing up, my waters broke and the C-section became an emergency; they would have to start straightway which left Andy insufficient time to arrive. The medical team were excellent and filmed the delivery. Samuel arrived into the world at 5.18 p.m. and Andy was wheeled in around eight minutes later. It was all very emotional. Although I would have loved for Andy to be there, I thank God that the appointments had run over and I happened to be connected to the monitor at just the right time and not driving home as I should have been. I can't imagine what would have happened if that were the case.

Samuel is such an outgoing, sociable and happy child. We feel that it may not be the right thing for us to have another child because of all the complexities in the mix, however he has four God brothers and lots of cousins with whom he is close. He is very sociable and I think all the comings and goings of carers means that he is actually well rounded as he has a strong relationship with lots of different people from many walks of life. Our live-in carers have known him since he was born and they share a special bond with him.

I don't think any family can provide a perfect upbringing for a child but I think if a child is loved and has stability then they can thrive. Other things within the mix may shape a child but there are positives and negatives to every family setup, and so we have to trust that God's grace will bridge the gaps. God did not plan for family units to live independently of him and outside of community with others; as the African proverb rightly attests, 'It takes a village to raise a child.' That being said, our situation is certainly not typical and there may be things that Samuel misses out on because of Andy's disability.

I don't want to gloss over the struggles that we still face daily. It has been hard for us to come to a new normal as a family of three rather than being a couple. Before having Samuel, Andy relied on me in so many ways and since Samuel arrived, naturally I haven't been able to support Andy in the same way – I know Andy has found this difficult.

There are also massive physical limitations on the relationship that Andy can have with Samuel. I know that this must pain Andy and cause frustration; it would be cliché to put into words how hard it is for him. Andy's facial expressions are limited and he also struggles to vary his tone of voice, things which are really important when interacting with a toddler. It is also difficult for Samuel to understand Andy's speech and so this limits conversation between them. The lion's share of the hands-on side of parenting is obviously down to me. It is hard for me to see Andy look on when we are playing, maybe in the park or on the beach, and I often wonder how Andy must feel. Andy can't be involved with simple things like kicking a football around with his son or picking him up if he falls over.

However, I am so thankful that there are many more areas in which Andy can be involved. It is lovely to spend time as a family and Dawlish has been a massive enabling factor for this. We also live next door to a park and there are lots of green spaces in the local area where we often take Samuel out on his bike and he and Daddy have races.

There are other ways that Andy's role as a father is imperative, a key factor being that Andy is still the breadwinner of the family by means of the insurance and pension that he had the foresight to put in place. He is also able to show the tough love that is needed when it comes to discipline and we are able to decide together the boundaries that we want to set.

We have been able to use various physical aids to facilitate Andy's connection with Samuel. When I was pregnant Andy had an idea to invent an attachment so Samuel's car seat could be locked onto his wheelchair and Samuel could bond with Andy. We also found a baby sling that worked really well so that Andy could hold his son. Samuel slept most soundly when he was tucked into Andy's arm; he could feel Andy's heartbeat and was snugly warm but of course Andy moving about wouldn't interrupt him!

As Samuel has grown, Andy has thought of new ways to relate to Samuel. He is able to use his electronic voice on his computer, for example, to back me up when Samuel isn't listening to me, and has a collection of phrases that he can play: 'Samuel, listen to Mummy', or 'Samuel, we don't talk like that', or 'Daddy loves you'. Samuel also likes to ride on Daddy's chair if we're out and about and he gets too tired to walk. Andy is the safe place that Samuel goes to when he needs quiet time – he calls this 'Daddy time' and it is an important part of his routine. Mostly they watch cartoons together but sometimes it might be a place where he can sit and do a quiet activity. Often this is a place where he falls asleep for a daytime nap. More recently, Samuel and Andy have enjoyed cooking together, where Andy will give the instruction from a recipe that he holds in his head.

I'm hoping that as Samuel grows he will learn many skills from Daddy. Since Andy's stroke I have completed many a task under his instruction, from rewiring a plug to soldering and other more complex DIY tasks. I envisage that Samuel will be following more and more of Andy's instructions to create and build as he grows. Most of all, with Andy showing incredible resilience in all areas of his life to achieve what he has, clinging onto his faith in spite of it all, I know that Samuel will grow to be very proud of his daddy and will learn so much from him.

11

About the Author (A Mother's Story)

'But we have this treasure in jars of clay to show that this all-surpassing power is from God and not from us. We are hard pressed on every side, but not crushed; perplexed, but not in despair; persecuted, but not abandoned; struck down, but not destroyed.' (2 Corinthians 4:7-9)

As I write this the entire world is in the grip of the Covid-19 pandemic and every single person is affected by the total life-change which this has brought to all men, women and children. We are all coming to terms with having 'a new normal' and lives which have been changed forever as we adjust our thinking, values and beliefs, trying to make sense of the chaos and confusion all around us. Such a time as this is unprecedented in its global impact on entire nations but the impact on the lives of individuals and families is unique to them, in their particular circumstances; they each have their own 'new normal' and the challenges this brings.

Having plenty of extra opportunities for reading, I picked up a book which I first read many years ago, *Leaning on a Spider's Web* by Jennifer Rees Larcombe. The blurb reads:

'The inhabitants of Laburnum Terrace are oblivious of the threat hanging over them. Living and loving, laughing and sometimes crying, they have built a world which seems comfortable and secure enough. But is it?'[1]

When the aircraft plunges from the sky at 5.00 a.m. one morning, the world of Laburnum Terrace is shattered to its core. The values on which the inhabitants have built their lives are put to the test, and some prove as fragile as spiders' webs.

The title is based on a passage of scripture:

'What they trust in is fragile; what they rely on is a spider's web. They lean on the web, but it gives way; they cling to it, but it does not hold.' (Job 8:14-15)

Until this pandemic hit our lives we were oblivious to the danger and disaster about to befall us all. We were all busy pursuing our own chosen lifestyles, trusting in our skills, talents and achievements, and placing value on the fragile, transient things in life. In these frightening times, with so many restrictions imposed on our normal routines and relationships, we need more than ever to rely on God, to trust him in all things and hold on to his promises. We all now have a 'new normal'.

As a family, our lives took on a 'new normal' from the day of Andrew's stroke in November 2011 but, as with the current crisis, the impact of that devastating episode on our lives has continually caused us to re-assess our priorities, beliefs and values. Despite the many challenges facing Andy, Emma, their extended family and friends

---

[1] Jennifer Rees Larcombe, *Leaning on a Spider's* Web (Hodder & Stoughton Religious, 1991).

over the past eight and a half years, we have tried to hold on to the promises of God:

> 'Have I not commanded you? Be strong and courageous. Do not be afraid; do not be discouraged, for the LORD your God will be with you wherever you go.' (Joshua 1:9)

God has said, 'Never will I leave you; never will I forsake you' (Hebrews 13:5).

Talking about the devastation and impact of the Coronavirus pandemic on the everyday lives of all people, Andy explained that little has changed for him personally but he thinks many people will now have a small window on how he thought his life would always be. Having been left with locked-in syndrome following his brain stem stroke, he is now tetraplegic, totally dependent on others for all personal care and mobility, seemingly isolated in his own body and his own home.

The four years following Andy's stroke are well documented in his first book *Pressed But Not Crushed*, charting his early struggles to regain the ability to speak, eat and move. Many hundreds of people prayed continuously for his healing but, as time went by and many therapies were employed, it seemed there was no significant improvement or healing. Andy was implored to spend more time in therapy, to seek new medical treatments, etc. However, God had a very different plan for Andy's life and we had to bring our prayers in line with God's purposes for him. We had to hold on to another of God's promises:

> "'For I know the plans I have for you," declares the LORD, "plans to prosper you and not to harm you, plans to give you hope and a future."' (Jeremiah 29:11)

Andy himself led the way to a change of emphasis in our prayers as he explained that he could spend several hours of every day in physical therapy and would never get back to 'normal' as his brain stem was badly damaged by the stroke; at best he may regain some limited movement. Andy decided that rather than focusing on all that he had lost, he would seek to use the many gifts and talents he had been given to benefit the lives of others as well as himself. He continues to this day to find new and innovative ways to use his brilliant mind, problem-solving skills and new technologies to keep pushing forward. What is truly miraculous is that he continues to be strong-willed and determined to surmount the myriad difficulties which assault him daily, to find solutions to problems and forge ahead exploring new possibilities and opportunities. As Andy declared recently, 'I think I am more useful to God as I am now than I ever was before.'

As a parent, and having watched my son grow to become the man he is today, I can now see God's hand on his life, preparing and enabling him to overcome and become the person he was created to be.

Andy was a very stubborn, determined toddler, prone to big tantrums when thwarted but was always ready to be loved and cuddled out of his unhappiness and frustration.

Although he was very late beginning to talk, it was obvious Andy understood most conversations and when he eventually spoke it was with a good use of language, in well-constructed sentences. It was also apparent that his mathematical concepts were well advanced for his age as he could easily calculate totals and differences at three years of age. However, his move to formal education did not go well as he struggled to read and write and was bored by the Early Years numeracy lessons, often misbehaving by singing loudly in class. Dyslexia was suspected but not diagnosed until he was much older, so Andy learned by reading poetry, which he could memorise, and sharing Enid Blyton's *Secret Seven* books with me. Meanwhile, Andy explored his interest in science, taught himself electronics and was able to build alarm systems and mend broken cassette recorders aged only eleven. He would wrestle with problems, thinking them through until he came up with solutions, some of which would come to him in dreams. Andy never gave up; he was never content with what he had achieved but quickly moved on to new challenges.

When he was five years old Andy became curious about God and Jesus. He had been part of a lively Sunday school at the Methodist church in our village; he had heard the well-known Bible stories and taken part in dramas and musicals. He asked one night what happened when people died and did they go to heaven! Keeping the words simple I explained that all people go to heaven to live with God if they believe in Jesus and ask him to help them. After thinking it over Andy asked if we could pray to Jesus. He committed himself to the Lord that night.

During the rest of his childhood and teenage years Andy became involved in many more church-based activities: cubs and scouts, Youth Fellowship, choir and drama. He threw himself wholeheartedly into everything he did, enthusiastically taking part in everything he could and relishing friendships and social interaction. Andy had to overcome the difficulties caused by asthma, making adventurous outdoor activities and sport particularly difficult. With great determination and stubbornness, nothing would stop Andy from aiming high, to be the strongest, fastest, part of the winning team in scouting expeditions and competitions.

Similarly, at high school he readily become involved in drama and musical performances, using his amazing ability to memorise words and scripts. His favourite subject at school was, surprisingly, not Maths or Science but English Literature. He revelled in the discussion and argument of texts in which he could express himself orally when writing was too difficult.

It wasn't until Andy began studying A levels that he found Maths and Science interesting and challenging, having theories to test and problems to solve. Having been to university open days he suddenly announced he wanted to study Dentistry and started looking at courses available to him. It became apparent that his A level subjects were not ideal as he was not studying Biology but rather Physics and Chemistry, as well as Maths and Further Maths.

Undaunted, Andy applied to various universities and was accepted by Birmingham University who pointed out that being dyslexic and lacking the all-important Biology qualifications could be problematical but they must have recognised his great strength of character and determination and offered him a place. Personally I believe Birmingham was the place God had plans for Andy's future but we could never have imagined what that future held for us all!

Having successfully achieved his ambition to become a dentist, Andy went on to be a clinical lecturer at the university, working at a dental drop-in centre and continuing his studies to gain further qualifications as well as working in general dental practice. He bought his own home, the car he'd always wanted and travelled abroad for even more adventurous outdoor activities. But at the same time Andy was drawn to know more about God and pursue his calling to follow Jesus and work for him in the church and the world. He re-committed his life to the Lord, being baptised in the Elim church and working as a youth leader. As with his professional life, Andy was driven to give everything he had in his work for the Lord, working in youth ministry and also outreach to addicts in Birmingham.

From the moment he met Emma, Andy knew she was the one for him; he called us the very next day to say he thought he had met the girl he was going to marry and, of course, he did! On their wedding day Pastor Stuart spoke about their marriage, quoting the Bible passage from the book of Ecclesiastes:

'Two are better than one, because they have a good return for their labour: if either of them falls down, one can help the other up. But pity anyone who falls and has no one to help them up. Also, if two lie down together, they will keep warm. But how can one keep warm alone? Though one may be overpowered, two can defend themselves. A cord of three strands is not quickly broken.' (Ecclesiastes 4:9-12)

What a blessing their union with each other and the Lord has been and continues to be, but that is their story to tell. For our part, as parents, we felt blessed to have such a wonderful Christian girl as Emma by our son's side.

Of course everything changed with Andy's stroke on 1st November 2011; the aftermath, the fight for life and the challenges of living with a severe disability are well documented in the book *Pressed But Not Crushed*. In the subsequent years since the publication of the book, Andy and Emma have had many distressing and frustrating times, many doubts and fears but also very many blessings. It has been these many blessings which have brought a wonderful reassurance and hope to Andy, Emma and all the family.

'"For I know the plans I have for you," declares the LORD, "plans to prosper you and not to harm you, plans to give you hope and a future."' (Jeremiah 29:11)

Although we have all hoped, prayed and anticipated a miraculous physical healing, it appeared that God wasn't answering our prayers as Andy remained paralysed and totally dependent on others for his physical needs. For me it was the words of the old hymn 'Count Your Blessings' which made me re-think my faith in God as a healer, sustainer and provider.

'When upon life's billows you are tempest-tossed,
When you are discouraged, thinking all is lost,
Count your many blessings, name them one by one,
And it will surprise you what the Lord has done.'[2]

Acknowledging the tremendous progress Andy has made and all he has achieved over the past nine and a half years, I fervently believe God is answering our prayers for healing as, miraculously, Andy presses on to live life to the fullest. I have seen the stubborn, determined little boy I once knew grow into a fine man using all the blessings, gifts and talents God has given him to forge ahead, overcoming the many obstacles which could have defeated him.

The list of Andy's achievements is breathtaking but his faith, courage and indomitable determination to overcome all obstacles is equally amazing.

Initially Andy was totally 'locked in', a prisoner in his totally useless body; he was on full life support, only able to move his eyes and blink once for 'yes', twice for 'no' in answer to questions. However, the reasoning, memory and intellectual parts of his brain were unaffected. He was aware that his life hung in the balance but when asked by Pastor Stuart if he wanted to fight for his life and everyone to pray for him, he responded with a very strong single blink. Andy believed – we all believed – that his healing and recovery were in God's hands and the 'angels' who treated and cared for him with such dedication. Indeed, he came out of the critical care unit within six days. Moving to a high dependency ward he began to regain his core strength, to move his head and mouth. He was determined to learn to eat and swallow once more, especially to be able to talk, but his limbs were totally useless. The only glimmer of hope was a small voluntary flicker of movement in his right

---

[2] Words: Johnson Oatman, Jr., 1856–1922 (Public Domain).

thumb. It was the combination of these few remaining abilities which were to effect the miraculous healing in not only Andy's life but all who surrounded him. A spiritual healing bringing us all into a much closer walk with God.

Those strangers who see Andy sitting in a wheelchair, unable to move and speak, can have no concept of the truly accomplished, intelligent and remarkable young man they see before them. He continues to keep his muscles and limbs moving through therapy and drug management but his main focus is in using the abilities and blessings he has been gifted by God. Using his considerable technological knowledge and skill (and his all-important right thumb) he has invested in all manner of hardware, software and devices which enable him to communicate, conduct business, manage his household and personal finances. His achievements to date include writing two books and completing a six-year course of study, graduating with a degree in Applied Theology. He has designed and organised the building of extensions and adaptions to their home, including an apartment for his live-in carers to have their own personal space. He researched and sourced an electric wheelchair, which has been adapted according to his instructions to be controlled by head movement and his trusty right thumb! The ability to leave his home and 'drive' himself around without a support assistant is a tremendous freedom. Andy has regained his speech which is very clear and easily understood by others when he is in a semi-reclined position at home, although sitting upright in his wheelchair outdoors is more of a challenge!

Every day is a challenge for Andy and Emma; many days have their triumphs over adversity but there are also many days when Andy's health deteriorates or he has a setback which threatens to defeat him. Andy's lungs have been damaged by the repeated chest infections caused by his inability to 'throw off' a cold or to cough voluntarily. Acknowledging he may have only a limited life left, Andy decided to celebrate in a big way, not only his actual birthday in October but also his second birthday in November. On the fifth anniversary of his stroke, 1st November 2016, Andy and Emma celebrated with a special meal, looking forward to new opportunities and adventures in the future. Their faith and courage were truly humbling given how we, his parents, were worrying that as another anniversary came around they would be depressed and pessimistic about the future. In my prayer journal that day I had written:

'Looking back and remembering only serves a purpose if we can recognise the purposes of God at work in our lives and be thankful for how he has brought us through troubling times.'

On 5th November 2011 I sent out an urgent plea to everyone I knew:

'Please, however tiny your faith, please pray. Don't hold back. Please pray for Andy, for his full recovery. We hold on to the promise of Jesus, "What is impossible with man is possible with God" (Luke 18:27). Please pray in whatever way you can that God will heal Andy and that our precious son will be restored to us, your prayers are so important to us.'

We can joyfully praise and glorify God, for he has indeed healed and restored our son to us. Andy's broken body belies the miraculous healing within; we can rejoice that he indeed has 'great treasure' within.

'But we have this treasure in jars of clay to show that this all-surpassing power is from God and not from us. We are hard pressed on every side, but not crushed; perplexed, but not in despair; persecuted but not abandoned; struck down, but not destroyed.'